YOUR KNOWLEDGE

- We will publish your bachelor's and master's thesis, essays and papers

- Your own eBook and book - sold worldwide in all relevant shops

- Earn money with each sale

Upload your text at www.GRIN.com and publish for free

Marc Backhaus

Sailing the Good Ship Albion on the Way to Arcady. Is Peter Doherty a Romantic Poet?

GRIN Publishing

Bibliographic information published by the German National Library:

The German National Library lists this publication in the National Bibliography; detailed bibliographic data are available on the Internet at http://dnb.dnb.de .

Imprint:

Copyright © 2015 GRIN Verlag, Open Publishing GmbH
Print and binding: Books on Demand GmbH, Norderstedt Germany
ISBN: 978-3-656-96687-6

This book at GRIN:

http://www.grin.com/en/e-book/300676/sailing-the-good-ship-albion-on-the-way-to-arcady-is-peter-doherty-a-romantic

GRIN - Your knowledge has value

Since its foundation in 1998, GRIN has specialized in publishing academic texts by students, college teachers and other academics as e-book and printed book. The website www.grin.com is an ideal platform for presenting term papers, final papers, scientific essays, dissertations and specialist books.

Visit us on the internet:

http://www.grin.com/

http://www.facebook.com/grincom

http://www.twitter.com/grin_com

Sailing the good ship Albion on the way to Arcady -

is Peter Doherty a Romantic Poet?

Bachelorarbeit

zur Erlangung des akademischen Grades

Bachelor of Arts (B.A.)

im Fach Englisch

Humboldt-Universität zu Berlin

Philosophische Fakultät II

Institut für Anglistik & Amerikanistik

eingereicht von Marc Backhaus

Berlin, den 14.04.2015

Table of Contents

Introduction   1

The Romantic Poet of Today
    i.   A Definition of English Romantic Poetry   3
    ii. Popular Rock Music as Heir to Romantic Poetry   16
    iii. Peter Doherty and his Romantic Public Persona   19
    iv. Peter Doherty and his Romantic Poetic Doctrines
        (a) Albion   24
        (b) Arcady   26

Lyric Analysis
    i.   Down for the Outing   29
    ii. The Ballad of Grimaldi   33
    iii. Albion   35
    iv. The Good Old Days   37

Conclusion   39

Appendices

Bibliography

Introduction

Peter Doherty is a poet of today whose form of expression is music. Devoting himself to being a "popstar [as well as] performance poet" (Doherty, *Books of Albion* 9), he is subject to extensive media coverage as a celebrity (cf. 262), on the one hand meticulously vituperated by the tabloid press for his junkie rocker lifestyle (cf. 141; Hannaford 158), on the other hand glorified as "a folk hero" (168), a "legend" (B Libertines 0:09:12) who "has come to epitomise British rock 'n' roll [...] as both pariah and idol" (Hannaford 3), "a true romantic with a God-given gift for melody and verse" (Pomphrey qtd. in 258) and even further as "the last of the Rock Romantics" (5).

Indeed, it can be argued that Doherty exercises a romanticizing of England as well as of his environment (cf. 60), and the issue of his work, in his own words "love, England & a quest for depth, grace & charm" (*Books of Albion* 19), is evocative of the emphasis on aestheticism, feeling, imagination and nationalism associated with English Romantic poetry (cf. "Romantic poetics"; "Romanticism" *Encyclopedia Britannica*). He employs in his works the themes of Albion and Arcady, glorifying a romanticised, idealised and imagined England with the first and in an escapist manner searching for liberty and infinity with the latter (cf. Yates & Samson 20-22; Black 109) – declaring Albion to be his and his band's "vessel" (qtd. in Hannaford 44) and their mission to "sail the good ship Albion to Arcadia" (qtd. in 44). This is strongly reminiscent of the remote-affine, idealist, symbolist, libertarian, nostalgic and visionary characteristics that compose English Romantic poetry as well as its stress on the sublime and the infinite (cf. Wu xxxvi-xxxix; Day 1, 2, 4, 172; Stewart 63; Goodman 195). Doherty proclaims:

> What you have with us is some people who can write some songs and, in the process, create another land. We have a romantic vision. We have a dream and, much to my surprise, it seems to be coming true. (qtd. in Black 20)

This statement can be considered a direct reenactment of the Romantics' thought that "they could create, through their writing, a promised land" (Wu xxxvii).

All of these observations lead to the interpretation that Peter Doherty certainly shares poetic doctrines with English Romantic poetry. Nonetheless, Doherty's public presentation and depiction as a Romantic, be it by himself or by the media, must also be taken into account. It is neither without significance nor reason that he is declared a Romantic on account of his philosophy (cf. Hannaford 229), lifestyle (cf. 231) and "self-destruction" (Anonymous Fan qtd. in 330), just as his

1

own frequent referencing and citing of the Romantic poets (cf. *From Albion to Shangri-La* 178), the placement of these in relation to Doherty by others (cf. B Libertines 0:08:46-0:09:19) and overall his depiction as well as self-depiction in interviews, books and in his published diaries. The question that therefore evidently arises is: Subjected to a lyric analysis[1], can Peter Doherty be termed a Romantic poet?

Bearing in mind Pattison's words that "rock has endowed the conventions of Romanticism with popular life" (38) and Hannaford's that Doherty has "revived the notion of the rockstar as intellectual and as romantic troubadour" (227), this bachelor paper will aim to answer this question by firstly providing a definition of English Romantic poetry and a justification as to why popular rock music can be considered heir to Romantic poetry, therefore why Doherty and his song lyrics can be subdued to a lyric poetry analysis, then by examining the depiction and perception of Doherty as a Romantic public persona and distinguishing this from his poetic doctrines that resemble those of the Romantic poet, Albion and Arcady. These two themes will be examined and put into literary context, whereupon the second part of this paper will comprise the lyric analysis of four of Doherty's songs with regard to the literary attributes that define Romantic poetry. Finally, a conclusion of all that has been found will close the paper, delivering an answer to the stated question.

Duncan Wu exclaims in the introduction to his anthology of Romanticism that Lord Byron was the first to enjoy the new-born "cult of celebrity" (xxxv) of the age, with "day-to-day reports of his affairs and adventures [filling] their [the gossip-columnists] pages. It is hard to imagine a poet now generating such speculation, or crowds of people following him through the streets" (xxxv). Peter Doherty is that poet – and this paper will conclude whether he can be ascribed to the same poetic movement as his predecessor.

---

1 The term 'lyric analysis' used in this paper describes the analysis of song lyrics by means of the tools of literary criticism used for analyzing lyric poetry as set out by Meyer and Wainwright.

The Romantic Poet of Today

i. A Definition of English Romantic Poetry

To begin with, a foundation for a definition of English Romantic poetry must be laid by briefly introducing Romanticism as a whole. *The Merriam-Webster Online Dictionary* defines Romanticism as

> **a** (1) : a literary, artistic and philosophical movement originating in the 18th century, characterized chiefly by a reaction against neoclassicism and an emphasis on the imagination and emotions, and marked especially in English literature by sensibility and the use of autobiographical material, an exaltation of the primitive and the common man, an appreciation of external nature, an interest in the remote, a predilection for melancholy, and the use in poetry of older verse forms [...]
>
> **b** : adherence to a romantic attitude or style. ("Romanticism")

The 5th edition of *The Oxford Companion to English Literature* adds that

> Intellectually it marked a violent reaction to the Enlightenment. Politically it was inspired by the revolutions in America and France . . . . Emotionally it expressed an extreme assertion of the self and the value of individual experience . . . together with the sense of the infinite and the transcendental. Socially it championed progressive causes . . . . The stylistic keynote of Romanticism is intensity, and its watchword is 'Imagination'. (Drabbe qtd. in Day 1)

It is important to note here that Romanticism is often described as a fluxionary movement and concept that "belongs to no period" (Wordsworth & Wordsworth xxiii) – despite its "centre of gravity [...] [being determined as] the end of the eighteenth century and the beginning of the nineteenth" (Day 4) – "and although many definitions are suggested, none command universal agreement" (Wu xxix). Romanticism is rather "an aspiring, a hopefulness – an exalting, and exulting, of the imagination" (Wordsworth & Wordsworth xxiii), a "mood in which 'we recognize / A grandeur in the beatings of the heart'" (xxiii), a term that describes a general, timeless movement without claiming universality of its elements (cf. Day 5). The German historical philosophical

3

dictionary *Historisches Wörterbuch der Philosophie* delineates this generality of Romanticism as the term's shift from its historical, chronologically assignable character to a transcendental, anthropological meaning (cf. "Romantik"). However, Paul O'Flinn argues in his book *How to Study Romantic Poetry* that "generalisations about Romanticism [...] are usually of doubtful worth" (8) as one cannot universalize "a range of voices saying different, often contradictory things" (6) – an argument confirming Wu's and Day's that a coherency of the elements of Romanticism across its voices is not implied, whilst it nevertheless remains a movement of transgressive, "fluid" (Wu xxix) character.

English Romantic poetry, though categorized according to its literary landmarks into roughly the same time span as Romanticism (cf. Wordsworth & Wordsworth xxiii-xxiv), is also assigned this fluid and transgressive character (cf. Chandler & McLane 3), mainly "because it speaks about a world that we not only recognise but also still inhabit" (O'Flinn 4) – or, in Harold Bloom's words: "For English-speaking readers, this age may be defined as extending from the childhood of Blake and Wordsworth to the present moment" (2), as "every fresh attempt of Modernism to go beyond Romanticism ends in the gradual realization of the Romantics' continued priority" (5).

Despite the therefore rather "over-systematising and simplifying" (Day 5) character of summaries of English Romantic poetry, many attempts are nevertheless made to define it, often within a more comprehensive than synoptic context which bears in mind that "Romantic assumptions evolve gradually, and over a length of time, before finding expression in the verse" (Wordsworth & Wordsworth xxvii). For instance, Harold Bloom, who distinguishes English from continental Romanticism by means of the English "native tradition of major poets writing in an ancestral mode" (3) and thus the English Romantic poets' "strong mutual conviction that they are reviving the true English tradition of poetry, which they thought had vanished" (3), terms English Romanticism and its poetry "a revival of romance" (3) and moreover "an internalization of romance, particularly of the quest variety" (3), from which follows that "the entire rhythm of the quest is heard again in the movement of the poet himself from poem to poem" (3). On this idea he bases his definition of two modes or phases of English Romantic poetry, the first called "Prometheus" (9) and the second "the Real Man, the Imagination" (9). The Prometheus phase is, according to Bloom, "marked by a deep involvement in political, social, and literary revolution, and a direct, even satirical attack on the institutional orthodoxies of [...] society [...] and the neoclassic literary and intellectual tradition" (9-10) – a description highly reminiscent of the definitions of Romanticism quoted above (see p. 3).

The Real Man, the Imagination, emerges after terrible crises in the major stage of the

4

Romantic quest, which is typified by a relative disengagement from revolutionary activism [...] so as to bring the search within the self and its ambiguities. In the Prometheus stage, the quest is allied to the libido's struggle against repressiveness, and nature is an ally, though always a wounded and sometimes a withdrawn one. In the Real Man, [...] nature is the immediate though not the ultimate antagonist. The final enemy to be overcome is a recalcitrance in the self, [...] the Selfhood. (10)

These movements of the English Romantic poet towards and away from nature as well as the self are what for Bloom constitutes the poet's development during his "internalization of quest-romance" (14) and he concludes for the Real Man, the Imagination, that

> [t]here are thus two main elements in the major phase of the Romantic quest, the first being the inward overcoming of the Selfhood's temptation, and the second the outward turning of the triumphant Imagination, free of further internalizations – though "outward" and "inward" become [...] false conceptual distinctions in this triumph, which must complete a dialectic of love by uniting the Imagination with its bride, who is a transformed ongoing creation of the Imagination rather than a redeemed nature. (16)

Adrian Day, who provides a chronological overview of constructions of the term Romantic, propounds interpretations of a development of English Romantic poetry similar to Bloom's proposition (which is taken into account as well). He quotes, for instance, Courthope, who claims that the Romantic poets "founded their matter and style on the principles to which that [French] Revolution gave birth" (qtd. in 88), yet defining for the poetry was "the translation of that external revolutionary energy into internal, 'spiritual' terms" (Dowden qtd. in 89). And

> Abrams' proposition [...] is that Romantic poets 'were all centrally political and social poets' [...] [who alongside] English radicals at the time of the French Revolution tended to interpret the Revolution in the light of the messianic, millenial, and apocalyptic framework of biblical prophecy. A renovated earth [...] was to be instituted through the Revolution. And poets declared themselves to be specially endowed with the capacity to envision this apocalypse. [...] Blake's elevation of the function of the poet to the role of the visionary bard was, Abrams continues, a typically Romantic move [...]. (Day 94-95)

5

This proposition highly resembles Bloom's Prometheus phase, and it is in Abrams' work that Day also explores what resembles Bloom's second phase, the Real Man, the Imagination. He demonstrates how Abrams distinguishes between two moods:

> 'The great Romantic poems were written not in the mood of revolutionary exaltation but in the later mood of revolutionary disillusionment or despair' [,] [...] disillusionment with historical reality [...]. (Day 97)

Day goes on to quote Abrams' proposition, made by means of an analysis of Wordsworth, that the English Romantic poets concluded from this disillusionment a "revelation" (qtd. in 98) concerning man's inherent qualities:

> Wordsworth evokes from the unbounded and hence impossible hopes in the French Revolution a central Romantic doctrine; one which reverses the cardinal neoclassic ideal of setting only accessible goals, by converting what had been man's tragic error – the inordinacy of his 'pride' that persists in setting infinite aims for finite man – into his specific glory and his triumph [...]. (qtd. in 98)

Abrams observes a shift of hope

> [...] from the history of mankind to the mind of the single individual, from militant external action to an imaginative act; and the marriage between the Lamb and the New Jerusalem has been converted into a marriage between subject and object, mind and nature, which creates a new world out of the old world of sense [...]. (qtd. in 99)

Very much like Bloom's interpretation of a dialectic of love between the Imagination and its creation (see quote p. 5), Abrams' interpretation sees "the dialectic between subject and object [...] and the hope of synthesizing the two terms of the dialectic [...] at the heart of Romanticism" (Day 105-106). However, in further examining "the Romantic symbolic mode" (110) that aims towards this synthesis, Day finds Paul de Man's critique to be that "Romanticism's claims to have found through symbolic language a means of uniting the subject, the self, in all its temporality, with a larger, often transcendental, object were a delusion" (121). Day continues by considering the work of Belsey, who sees "the self-cancelling logic of Romantic dreams of reconciling subject and the object in a way which gives priority to the subject" (121) and claims that it is "the heroic impossibility of this task which produces Romantic exultation and despair" (qtd. in 121). Finally, Day observes that

> [i]n the wake of de Man's essay numerous critics in the 1970s and 1980s began to interpret the basic strategy of Romantic poetry as one in which the poets sought to evade recognition simultaneously of their own temporality and the temporality of the language within which the self is constituted. (122)

It is "the self-referential, self-mystifying, self-transcendentalizing Romantic ideology advanced by the mature Wordsworth or Coleridge" (Day 161), "this focus on and celebration of subjectivity that is sometimes seen as the distinctive Romantic innovation" (47), yet the self's transcendence remains an unattainable goal.

Wordsworth & Wordsworth determine the development of English Romantic poetry and its "ideals, values and belief" (xxvii) as a process initiated by reaction against "neo-classicism and the Age of Reason" (xxvii), "but at a secondary stage a new optimism, a new momentum, is created that is forward-looking, positive in itself" (xxvii). They suggest that

> [t]he optimism (or naivity) to be seen in this keeping faith with the Revolution is a major characteristic of the earlier Romantic poets. They have both to come to terms with disappointment, and to quell disillusion by finding an apolitical basis for confidence in humanity and hope for the future. To some it seemed at first that Godwin's faith in reason might provide the answer, but instinctively they were drawn rather to feeling and imagination. (xxix)

Whilst in this aspect Wordsworth & Wordsworth's proposition resembles those of Bloom and Abrams, it differs in their distinction not between two phases or moods, but between two generations of English Romantic poetry when placing the poets into historical context. The first generation, embodied by "Smith, Burns, Robinson, Blake, Southey, Coleridge & Wordsworth" (xli) and assigned to the time span between 1786 and the end of the 1790s (cf. xxxv, xli), is marked by the revolutionary optimism depicted above (see quote) and its poets, "at times openly millenarian [...] [,] view man as godlike in his potential. Their theme is imagination" (xli). The second generation, emerging after a "gap [...] widened by the fact that so little major poetry was published between 1800 and 1810" (xxxix), lack this optimism (cf. xli). Instead, these poets (namely "Byron,

Shelley, Hunt, Hemans, Keats, Landon and Hood" (xli)) distance themselves from the subjects of revolution, the lower and working class (cf. xlii) and write poems whose "solipsistic beauty shares with no one, values only the moods of the writer" (xlii) – an interpretation that can be regarded as an alternative parallel to Bloom's interpretation of the internalization of romance and movement towards the self.

Bearing all of these propositions for definitions of English Romantic poetry in mind, it can be ascertained that they all share the observation of an internalization of revolutionary doctrines, a conversion of these, as it were, into an exaltation of the single individual and the imagination, of their boundlessness in potential, and furthermore a development of striving towards the unity of the subject, the mind, the imagination, and the object, nature, imagination's product.

On the one hand, English Romantic poetry is defined as an ongoing, transgressive development which "denotes not just a period, but a style, a movement, a way of thinking […], even a way of being in the world" (Chandler & McLane 3), so that "poets writing long after the Battle of Waterloo might well think of themselves as 'in the Romantic line'" (3) – and, having demonstrated that Romanticism and "the literature of the period has been ceaselessly reinterpreted and reconstructed" (Day 202) throughout the time that comes after it, Day concludes in his work that this "is not surprising" (202), as it has been done "by later commentators who have themselves only been ringing the changes on paradigms laid down in the period itself" (202). Wordsworth & Wordsworth put it this way: "our version of the Romantic period is a reflection of our taste, not that of the time" (xl), Chandler & McLane additionally suggest that "Romantic poetry, however deeply rooted in its historical and cultural moment, also remains 'ever more about to be,' […] ever ready to be reactivated and reimagined by the latest reader" (8).

On the other hand, the considered propositions and observations nevertheless claim to lay down set attributes and literary features of English Romantic poetry. And in addition to the exultation of the limitless imagination and individual, the shift of revolutionary hope from society to the single mind, the poet as "visionary bard" (Day 95), the "dialectic of love" (Bloom 16) between man, or the imagination, and his counterpart, or its creation, the use of symbolism, and the quest for non-temporality, or infinity, as well as the attributes listed in the dictionaries (see p. 3), the works that aim to define English Romantic poetry specify several further attributes, which shall in the following paragraphs also be taken into consideration.

To stay in line with the adaptation and conversion of revolutionary doctrines in English Romantic poetry, the first further literary attribute considered here is laid out by Frye, who claims that

Romanticism and its poetry were "primarily a revolution in poetic imagery" (qtd. in Day 101):

> What I see first of all in Romanticism is the effect of a profound change, not in belief, but in the spatial projection of reality. This in turn leads to a different localizing of the various levels of that reality. . . .
>
> the metaphorical structure of Romantic poetry tends to move inside and downward instead of outside and upward, hence the creative world is deep within, and so is heaven or the place of the presence of God. [...] In the Romantic construct there is a center where inward and outward manifestations of a common motion and spirit are unified, where the ego is identified as itself because it is also identified with something which is not itself. (qtd. in Day 102-103)

Frye gives examples of this 'metaphorical structure' in several Romantic poems' depictions of worlds and constructs situated "underneath experience" (qtd. in Day 102), "down" (qtd. in 102), coming "from below" (qtd. in 103), and "at the deep center" (qtd. in 103) – as opposed to the structures of heaven and grace as outward influences in pre-Romantic poetry (cf. 103).

Secondly, Wordsworth & Wordsworth observe a "Romantic Platonism" (xxxii) and Unitarianism (cf. xxxii), acted out and proclaimed especially by Coleridge (cf. xxxii-xxxv), who "sought ways of understanding the 'unity of consciousness'" (xxxiii) and stated

> [...] that the Great Invisible is 'by symbols seen', that it is our task to read the Book of Nature, interpret the 'eternal language that [our] God utters'. It is this [...] implication that gives to Coleridge his lifelong preoccupation with imagination – the power that [...] enables us to perceive the godhead, and perceive ourselves at one with it. 'Tis the sublime of man' [...]. (xxxiv)

"Romantic treatments of the sublime as that which exceeds formulation and representation, that which signifies transcendence" (Day 163) as well as "the self's own sublime potential" (163) are in English Romantic poetry linked to a sense of and search for eternity as well as infinity: in the Platonic and Unitarian line, Blake states that "If the doors of perception were cleansed, everything would appear to man as it is, infinite" (qtd. in Wordsworth & Wordsworth xxxiv). Wordsworth & Wordsworth collaterally suggest that "man would regain the lost fourfold vision of eternity" (xxxiv) and add Wordsworth's idea that "imagination was associated with an 'obscure sense of possible sublimity'" (xxxiv). Day observes that "Burke found the sublime in anything earthly that could produce the impression of infinity: in natural phenomena and in human constructions whose dimensions, particularly along the vertical line, are huge and grand" (184), and proposes himself that "the capacity to apprehend the absolute is frequently referred to by the Romantics with the term imagination, just as the term imagination is often used to define the absolute itself" (59). For Day, "the tension between subject and object in Romantic writing is resolved in an idealist fashion through the positing of an ultimate correlation between the individual mind and the mind of the absolute" (59) – in a quest to reconcile contraries (cf. 58).

Within this context, the English Romantic poet's self-assigned role as "visionary bard" (Day 95) is again constructed, and Abrams defines it as follows:

> In many poems the Romantics do not write direct political and moral commentary but [...] 'politics of vision', uttered in the persona of the inspired prophet-priest. [...] the Romantic Bard is one 'who present, past, and future sees'; so that in dealing with current affairs his procedure is often panoramic, his stage cosmic, his agents quasi-mythological, and his logic of events apocalyptic. Typically this mode of Romantic vision fuses history, politics, philosophy, and religion into one grand design, by asserting Providence – or some form of natural teleology – to operate in the seeming chaos of human history so as to effect from present evil a greater good; [...] the French Revolution functions as the symptom [...] of the abrupt culmination of this design, from which will emerge a new man on a new earth which is a restored Paradise. (qtd. in Day 95-96)

Furthermore, a sense of "cultural nationalism" (Chandler & McLane 4) is observed in English Romantic poetry. Chandler & McLane term this "ethnopoetics" (5):

> In addition to, or entwined with, a poetry-of-consciousness, or reflexive subjectivity, Romantic poetry emerges as a project of cultural enquiry, national fantasy, and sociopolitical critique as much as a poetry of self and nature: ethnopoetics meets psychology in this period in ways that still shape our own. (5)

Wordsworth & Wordsworth similarly take note, under the sub-heading "A New Style and a New Spirit" (xxx), of a "primitivist view of poetry as naturalness [...] being advanced" (xxx) before English Romantic poetry, "stirred by patriotism etc. 'the ancient bard arose and sang . . . native effusions of the heart'" (xxx), a view that is adopted by the Romantic poets who follow, yet modified to fit the contemporary world:

> The difference between the primitivist critic and the Romantic poet is that Blair [...] continues to think in terms of a distant past, Wordsworth looks through similar eyes at the 'solitary rural scenes' of contemporary England. (xxxi)

This suggestion can be understood as the English Romantic poets' celebration of a cultural nationalism based on national history, yet transferred onto contemporary life in England.

The aspect of "cultural enquiry [...] [and] national fantasy" (Chandler & McLane 5) leads directly on to another feature of English Romantic poetry "so frequently associated [with Romanticism] as to be nearly synonymous" (Goodman 195) – the predilection for nostalgia. Quoting Wordsworth's claim that "Poetry is passion: it is the history or science of feelings" (qtd. in 195) to introduce his work, Goodman characterizes today's view of romantic nostalgia, worth quoting at length, and he begins with listing the "many returns associated with the [Romantic] period" (195):

> [...] its "nostalgia for the natural object, expanding to become nostalgia for the origin of this object," the longing for nature [,] [...] the retrieval of romance modes, the renewed interest or imaginative investment in national and cultural pasts, the turn from polite culture to the "very language of men" [...] and the reanimation of oral cultures and orality [...]. The [...] understanding of nostalgia in each case casts the phenomenon as a distancing, even a falsification, of the pressing realities of modernity: urbanization, the vexed national politics within a newly but uneasily united kingdom of Britain, the equally if not more vexed international marketplace. This is the nostalgia familiar [...] today – the sentimental and safe retrospect, the pleasing melancholy, the whitewashing of less lovable aspects of history, past and present alike. Susan Stewart thus writes that nostalgia testifies to "a longing that of necessity is inauthentic . . . because the past it seeks has never existed except in narrative." The nostalgic, she writes, "is enamored of distance, not of the referent itself." Nostalgia, writes one critic of postmodernity, "exiles us from the present as it brings the imagined past near"; another, Frederic Jameson, argues that nostalgia [...] is "an elaborated symptom of the waning of our historicity, of our lived possibility of experiencing history in some active way." (195)

11

Goodman argues that in the Romantic period (which he assigns to the 18th and early 19th century (cf. 196)) however, nostalgia was defined rather as a scientific disease triggered by displacement through warfare, colonialism as well as forced travel (cf. 196) and characterized, contrarily to today's view, by "the growing pains of historical existence" (196). He goes on to state his proposition that, in the course of the emergence of English Romantic poetry, the "new 'home' for the historical disease […] [came to lie] in Romantic-era writings on aesthetics. More specifically, it came to reside in the period's discourse about Poetry" (197), in the sense that "the history of mobility – and history perceived as motion – came to lodge in the project and practice of poetry itself" (199). Goodman finds, in analyzing Wordsworth's "The Thorn", that "the effects of nostalgia are no longer just a subject of representation – they have become a defining principle of representation" (206), and that the scientific disease nostalgia finds a "lineal descendant here, in that 'craving of the mind [...]'" (207) practiced by the Romantic poets, who seemingly aim to

> […] make craving nostalgics of us all – that is, to correct our eyes from skimming the 'space upon paper' by catching our minds in the same repetitive motion to induce or encourage thought's tendency to return to the same grooves […]. (207)

The return to these 'grooves' is, according to Goodman, in other words characterized as "a mindfulness of the affective weight ('balance of feelings') rather than the semantic or informational content of words" (207), and he elaborates that "words as things are [in English Romantic poetry] preferred to words valued for their exchangeability – [...] as 'symbols of the passion' […] [rather than] as spaces on the paper" (208). It can in other words be said that nostalgia in English Romantic poetry is coupled, like its Platonism, Unitarianism, exaltation of imagination and search for unity, with a strong affinity for symbolism as well as aestheticism. The Romantic poem, "according to Wordsworth, seeks both to recreate and to induce by means of tautology and other forms of repetition or repetitive motion" (208) – a literary feature Goodman terms "the arrested locomotion – the logo-motion" (208). He suggests that it is "the pathos of motion, or a certain kind of endless, unfree motion" (208) that has been transmuted from the scientific understanding of a disease into "poetic motion[,] […] the motion simulated and induced by the poem and the techniques of the meter, which contribute, along with other verbal effects, to that overall motion" (209).

The meter, poetic form and style of English Romantic poetry are in fact also determined and defined in detail. Whilst Wordsworth & Wordsworth synoptically speak of "extreme simplicity of language and openness of emotion" (xxx) along with "tenderness and sublimity" (Blair qtd. in xxx) as "the

12

characteristics of this style" (xxx), and Chandler & McLane generically take note of "a sense of verbal electricity in Romantic poetry" (1) – the poet becoming "on Shelley's account a kind of modern Prometheus, a poet of the electric life of words" (1), Susan Stewart offers an elaborate contextualization of Romantic meter and form, which is, according to her, essentially selected and applied to carry into effect one objective – the "transformations of feeling" (57).

Stewart states that the "themes [of Romanticism] were expressed in meters and forms of great variety – some reach back to antiquity, others were newly invented, and many were put to new occasions and uses" (54), and an overall "contrary reaction against any excessive regularity" (56) goes hand in hand with "the contention that the content of the work should determine the shape of the form" (57) already emerging by the middle of the 18th century (cf. 57). In this light, Stewart points out the "effects of musical mimesis" (57) observable in English Romantic poetry:

> The Romantic critique of eighteenth-century syllabic prosody was based not only in an idea about fidelity to the passions, but as well [...] about fidelity to expression [...] [;] poetry was to represent the emotions and not to be an ideal and regulating force upon them; to this extent, arguments about poetic representation followed arguments about musical representation and led poets to become interested in the equal-time principles of accentual verse that linked the metrical foot with the musical bar. (58)

Stewart names the example of "chanting as a device of Romantic poetic composition" (58), then goes on to examine Wordsworth's ideas on the selective use of irregularity and regularity in poetic meter to achieve certain aims – "the regularity of a meter might sustain a poet expressing a nearly inexpressible content; the irregularity of meter might enliven and complicate a single thought" (72) – and this bears the "sense that poets could make a painful content bearable by means of metrical ease: 'The end of Poetry is to produce excitement in co-existence with an overbalance of pleasure'" (59).

Under the sub-heading "Native sources" (60), Stewart elucidates how "Poets in the second half of the eighteenth century and the beginning of the nineteenth tended to turn to [...] British roots for their practice" (60), among which were "stately enjambed blank verse" (60) and traditional "British ballad forms" (60) in which "the character of the nation displays itself in striking colours" (Cowper qtd. in 60), and

> [...] the poets [...], confronted by the crisis in audience that the popularity of the

13

novel, the extension of literacy, and the decline of local traditions and patronage posed, looked variously to the English, Welsh, Scots, and Irish minstrels, bards, and ballad-singers for models of their craft [...] since song forms untied many of the knots presented by the eighteenth-century prohibition on trisyllabic 'substitutions.' (60)

Examples of this are for Stewart given in the "'Burns meter' [derived from the old Scotch Songs], [...] a six-line stanza form using a tail rhyme, or rhyme that unites the stanzas" (60), the use of Scottish meter "derived from troubadour tradition" (61), of "medieval Irish accentual verse" (61) as well as of the "effects of trisyllabic and trochaic substitution" (61), a "widespread interest in hymns" (61), "permutations on ballad, hymn, and common meter" (62), "broadside ballads" (62), borrowings from "classical epic, such as heroic epiphets, hyperbole, and hyperbata" (63), and overall in the "Romantic aesthetic of poetic sublimity, inspired by nature and techniques of heightened rhetoric and intense meter at once" (63). "The influences of Milton and Spencer, along with British song traditions, transformed a syllabic and heroic predilection to an accentual and lyric one" (63), Stewart concludes.

Furthermore, Stewart outlines the English Romantic poets' turn to "Ancient sources" (63), among which are "the rules of symmetry and heroic narrative in the dactylic hexameters of epic verse and the distiches of elegiacs" (63), the "uneven lines and stanza forms of Pindar's odes, the pounding heterometric stanzas of Sappho, Horace's practice of [...] widely varying verse forms" (63), "complex ambiguous syntax" (63) in line with Horatian forms, "pronounced pauses" (63), in fact a turn especially to "Greek and Roman models" (64). Yet additionally, the "Romantics were [also] able to read their own aesthetics back into neoclassical works" (64). Stewart further introduces the Hebrew Bible as another "important model for poetic form [...] [in its] use of anaphora, syntactical parallelism, catalogues, and doubled sequences of phrases or clauses" (64) as well as its

> [...] major genres [...] – the epithalamia [...], the hymns, the narrative poems of prophecy and the suffering of Job; the dirges on the destruction of Jerusalem in Lamentations and the aphorisms in Proverbs and Ecclesiastes [...]. (65)

Interpreting into Blake's "Jerusalem" an adoption of these poetic genres, Stewart observes a "focusing upon the meaning of a medial caesura that organizes a paradoxical relation between nothing and becoming nothing, withdrawing and releasing" (65) – and demonstrates with this example a direct link in English Romantic poetry between the use of rhyme and meter and the transformation of the poem's content. She further finds that "Byron's use of discontinuous rhythm [...] is another innovation" (66), and all in all concludes a "syncretic dimension of Romantic meter and form" (66) that borrows, imitates and varies between different sources and models – an "age of prosodic simplicity gave way to an age of great prosodic texture [...] [in which] the liberty of the poet to choose a form increased" (66). Ancillary "accentual inventions" (67) are from Stewart's point of view spearheaded by the important influence Chatterton (cf. 67) with his "astonishing inventiveness" (67) of new stanza forms, his ten-line poems, inter alia, which served as examples for the later English Romantic poets' odes (cf. 67), as well as "his facility with meter" (67); also, "the conversation poem" (69) emerges from traditional British ballad "call-and-response structures" (68) as the Romantic poets develop a "tendency [...] to ask questions in their poems" (69).

> The metrical romance, a poem situated in the margin between history and the imagination, allows for effects of surprise and drama to be heightened by the regularity of its beats. (69)

And as regards content, the

> [...] demands the Romantic poets place on contexts of landscape and weather in their meditative odes are heavy and give evidence of poets who cannot fall back on the ritual structures of social life to put into motion traditional meanings for poetry or for existence. Romantic poetry faced the need to generate its own occasions, and this alone may explain why so much of it was about poetry itself. (70)

To conclude her work, Stewart finds that the "story of Romantic meter and form is often told within a liberation narrative that is rooted in Romanticism itself" (72) and argues that

> [...] perhaps the most important and universal legacy of their work in theory and practice [...] [is that they] created a domain where theory and practice are one as they insisted upon yoking conceptual and sensual life in the production of form. (72)

Finally, Chandler & McLane, examining Wordsworth's "The World is Too Much With Us", claim to capture the author

> [...] in what might be described as a quintessentially Romantic moment, catching

himself in the act of wishing himself out of enlightenment, into re-enchantment, but just by virtue of having to wish it so, he acknowledges that the customary creed of the ancients cannot simply be put on again as if nothing had happened since. [...] But how interesting that he frames his wish to reinhabit this creed in terms of alternative siblings. These are the two sons of Poseidon [...] [who] suggest the double-sidedness of *poiesis*, a duality the Romantics compulsively explored. Able to inhabit any form, Proteus [...] [is the] elastic conception of poetry as any great imaginative achievement, [...] Triton [...] [is] 'poetry in a more restricted sense', that is, metrical language. (6)

In conclusion of all that has been taken into account, English Romantic poetry is indeed thoroughly defined in the numerous literary features and attributes its critics observe, whilst the claim of their universality is still not made. All set and laid out features do seem to share one doctrine, though: the liberty of the Romantic mind, the Romantic poet, and the exaltation of that liberty hand in hand with the Romantic poet's expression and his imagination. English Romantic poetry is also by all considered critics acknowledged as an ongoing development that adopts and reinterprets doctrines of the past, and whose own doctrines still influence us today. It is this latter aspect that leads on to the next sub-chapter of this paper, which will investigate how popular rock music is seen as heir to Romantic poetry.

ii. Popular Rock Music as Heir to Romantic Poetry

The first sense in which British popular music as such is considered heir to English Romantic poetry is in its role as "primary signifier and expression of contemporary national identity" (Morra 10). Morra argues in her work that

> [a]s reinforced and promoted in a mainstream media, in national celebrations, in television and film, and at times in popular music itself, [...] [p]opular music now claims a contemporary national and cultural role akin to that hitherto occupied by English literature. (10)

She observes in the works of various critics the description of a very "dominant contemporary [...] call for enquiry" (3) for an assertion of Britishness, of a British national and cultural identity, amidst a "'crisis of English identity' [...] made worse by the fact that the English 'have never developed a sufficiently democratic narrative of their national identity" (3). Morra quotes, inter alia, Kumar, who asserts that "[a]ll that the English can really call upon is the highly selective, partly nostalgic and backward-looking version of 'cultural Englishness' elaborated in the late nineteenth century and continued into the next" (qtd. in 4), finds Easthope to "argue that Englishness is in fact identifiable [...] [and] best evidenced in defining literary enterprises" (5), other critics to "acknowledge in communal performance and popular forms (sport, film, festivals) a defining contemporary significance" (6), yet "none of the major cultural histories [to contemplate] music as a significant voice" (6). It is Morra herself – pointing out that her "approach merely reflects a common critical assumption that Englishness must be located within established cultural practices or expressions" (8) – who acknowledges British popular music's "very real *national* role" (9) as claimed by the mainstream media (see quote above), explaining that "popular music is variously [...] received as an implicit response to the cultural void necessitated by the 'decline' of English literature" (11).

Within this context, not only the "cultural enquiry [...] [and] national fantasy" (Chandler & McLane 5) of English Romantic poetry come to mind, but also

> [...] the role that Romantic poetry has played in the development of modern criticism and of 'English' as an academic discipline. The fate of Romantic poetry as a field of study has been closely tied to the fate of literary studies [...].
>
> (Chandler & McLane 3)

As Chandler & McLane observe in "anthologies of British poetry or British literature [...] [that] the quantity of pages given to Romantic poets is out of all proportion to its brevity in years" (2), they point out "how elevated a position poetry had in the hierarchy of cultural practice for Britain in this period" (2). Thus, following Morra's suggestion, English Romantic poetry can be seen as a major component of the predecessor of British popular music, namely British literature, and moreover it can be asserted that the main art in the 'hierarchy of cultural practice for Britain' has shifted from poetry in the Romantic period to popular music today. It therefore appears justified to exercise a literary analysis of a popular musician's lyrics of today, in this paper's case Peter Doherty's, and compare his works to English Romantic poetry, of which they are, to a certain extent, heir.

The second sense in which this heritage is proposed is thoroughly elaborated by Pattison as "the triumph of vulgarity" (3) adopted from Romanticism by rock music:

An investigation of rock's origins shows that Romanticism is a living popular creed, not a superannuated artistic movement; that this creed, originally the province of an educated minority, is now by mutation the ideological currency of the Western masses; and that beneath the primitive rhythms of rock is a vulgar pantheism, the unacknowledged mass creed of which Romanticism and its popular music are harbingers. (30)

Pattison sees in vulgarity the main literary, musical and cultural element that has been passed on from Romantic poetry to rock music, or rather expropriated by the latter and made its own (cf. vi). He proposes that "[n]ineteenth-century Romanticism lives on in the mass culture of the twentieth century" (xi), especially in rock music:

Rock is appealing because it's vulgar, and an appreciation of it requires a defense of vulgarity [, which] is implicit in the Romanticism and pantheism that have been staples of refined culture for the last two hundred years [...]. The triumph of vulgarity does not mean the extermination of elite culture but the reinterpretation of that culture in a popular mode. [...] [R]ock expropriates Romanticism's refined traditions of self, sex, science, and social organization [...]. (v-vi)

In his claim Pattison clearly acknowledges Romanticism's ongoing influence as a 'living popular creed' and sees its doctrines reinterpreted by rock music. Though he explicitly focuses on American rock music (cf. x), he regards it as heir to the Romantic period in Britain and Europe, observing that as "[t]he Romantic revolution has posed vulgarity as a central question for the modern period" (14), "America has perfected the rites of vulgar Romantic pantheism. [...] And the music of its ritual is rock" (29). He goes as far as to elevate rock as "the progress of Romanticism" (38):

Rock adopts the Romantic notion of the primitive as the cornerstone of its mythology and takes over the Romantic conventions associated with it. [...] But rock goes two extra steps. Rock has made Romanticism available in a populist formula [...], and rock offers this populist Romanticism not just as a network of artistic conventions but as a living creed. (38)

Pattison's work, focused on American rock music, gains in relevance for British rock music in light of Barnes' similar but reversed claim that

[...] the Romantic poets were the rock stars of their day. They didn't want to be part of mainstream society and, as such, toyed with both drugs and death. But the mainstream just couldn't leave them alone. Barnes says these poets played a social role. (Hannaford 231)

It jumps at the eye in these observations that their authors seemingly assert an interfacing bridge between the literary and cultural attributes of Romanticism that allows for Romantic doctrines to be carried onto today's popular rock music as, in Pattison's words, a "living creed" (38). The aim of this paper is to evaluate whether Peter Doherty can be termed a Romantic poet by means of a literary analysis of his lyrics. It is therefore necessary beforehand to distinguish between the literary attributes of his work and his cultural, popular attributes as a Romantic in the sense that Morra, Pattison and Barnes suggest, in other words the depiction and perception of Doherty as a Romantic on account of and through his public persona. This distinction will be the subject of the next two sub-chapters, beginning with the latter.

iii. Peter Doherty and his Romantic Public Persona

Critical and commercial successes the Libertines, and Pete's follow up project Babyshambles were drenched in lager soaked romanticism, and nuances of 21st century city living – often imitated never bettered. With partner in crime Carl Barat, Doherty kick started a cultural revolution redefining indie rock for years to come.

("Pete Doherty Live Show: Brixton Jamm")

It seems that in his book *Peter Doherty: Last of the Rock Romantics*, Alex Hannaford portrays Peter Doherty as the personification of Pattison's suggestion of rock's conversion of Romanticism's doctrines into a living creed. He observes "the myth of Pete Doherty" (5), who is described as "very much a poet with a romanticised view of life [...] [,] a fantasist" (Bourcier qtd. in 68), a "carefree minstrel playing songs where and when he pleases amongst adoring fans" (*NME* qtd. in 155), who has, in Hannaford's own words, "revived the notion of the rock star as intellectual and as romantic troubadour" (227). From these statements it already becomes clear that Doherty's medial presence and public persona act as the source on which his attribution to Romanticism is based. Hannaford quotes an anonymous fan who reveals to "like the romanticism of his self-destruction" (qtd. in 330), and after introducing Barnes' proposition on the Romantic poets as "the rock stars of their day"

(231), he places the "drama of ostracism" (Barnes qtd. in 231) exerted by the media upon Doherty in direct comparison. Hannaford furthermore takes into account the English Romantic poets' inclination to take drugs "to endure the living" (233) in relation to Doherty's drug abuse, as well as Doherty's biography, which, he claims, shows a fascination and idealization of the working class equally exerted by the Romantic poets (cf. 228-229). It is Doherty's libertarian lifestyle, equated by himself with "freedom" (337), with which he for Hannaford "embodies the mythology of the iconic musician [...] [, becoming] an outlaw in rock 'n' roll" (338); it is his realized living as "a wandering minstrel who felt such a closeness to his fans he'd invite them home to hear his music [...] [and] his poetry" (340) which constructs Doherty as a "rock romantic" (340). Matilda Battersby shares this proposition, seeing in Doherty's "wish to emulate the bohemian ideal" and in his presentation "a new romantic, a poet and a rebel".

This association of Doherty as a rock musician with Romanticism in terms of a living creed is not only inarguably in line with Pattison's proposition, but also reinforced by what can be observed as Doherty's own referencing and citing of Romantic poets as well as the placement of these in relation to him by others. The inclusion of a painting based on "The Death of Chatterton" by Henry Wallis (1856) on the cover of the Babyshambles album "Shotter's Nation"[2] can not be regarded as insignificant for Doherty's self-presentation and the presentation of his songs as in some respect connected and related to English Romantic poetry, nor can the same be done with his quoting of Wordsworth in his published diaries (cf. *From Albion to Shangri-La* 178). A documentary on Doherty published on YouTube by B Libertines uses the means of audiovisual presentation to bring into contextual correlation the public persona of Doherty and quotes from Baudelaire[3] – who is seen "as a crucial link between Romanticism and modernism" ("Charles Baudelaire") – as well as Byron:

> In him inexplicably mixed appeared much to be loved and hated, sought and feared.
> Opinion varying o'er his hidden lot, in praise or railing ne'er his name forgot.
>
> (0:08:45-0:09:20)[4]

It is this quote, taken from the English Romantic poet and used within this new context to describe the characteristics of the public persona of Peter Doherty, that leads on to a further fundamental

---

2 see Appendix A, Figure 1.
3 The quote of Baudelaire, displayed in the documentary without punctuation, is: "So that you may not be the martyred slaves of time you must get intoxicated, get intoxicated and never pause for rest with wine, poetry or virtue as you choose" (B Libertines 0:01:05-0:01:46), evidently bringing into connection with Doherty a living creed very much reminiscent of the Romantic poetic doctrines (see *i. A Definition of English Romantic Poetry*).
4 The quote is, as with Baudelaire's, displayed in the documentary without punctuation.

aspect of that public persona, best delineated by himself:

> It's not a persona. I was very much isolated all the time; it's just the world I lived in. It just comes from my imagination. Just cellotaping together loads of dilletantes fantasies and see if you can actually live the poetry that you write [...].
>
> *(Move* qtd. in *Books of Albion* 132)

And the 'poetry' that he attempts to 'live out' greatly resembles the poetic doctrines of English Romantic poetry, though several other influences are mentioned, among which are the libertine:

> To find contemporary resonances of Arthur Rimbaud we don't have to look very far. Pete Doherty's drug fuelled creativity is on the front of tabloids [...] and on television in everything from the national news to the late review. [...] Doherty's output as an artist is over shadowed by the overwhelming interest in his activity as a celebrity, and in this respect he differs greatly from his 19th century counterpart.
>
> (unknown qtd. in Doherty, *Books of Albion* 262)

Further of his indicated role models are the Marquis de Sade (cf. Yates & Samson 24-25), Oscar Wilde (cf. 38), George Orwell (cf. 38), Paul Verlaine (cf. Doherty, *Books of Albion* 132), 1960s British television and especially Tony Hancock (cf. Hannaford 29, 42), The Smiths (cf. 32), yet indeed also the English Romantic poets (cf. 20), and in light of the claims of "the Romantics' continued priority" (Bloom 5), these influences can be interpreted as ongoing developments of Romantic doctrines.

Doherty's attempt at poetry lived out finds itself expressed in his published diaries and quotes in phrases among which are "The stress of Longing" (*Books of Albion* 12), "The past & the future are contaminated with doubt & nostalgia. The insuperable oblivion was voluntary" (109), "I do crave the loneliness' grave" (158), "I must soon take it & run [...] to truly follow my heart & the melody of the stark & in turns calamitous & divine betrayal of either: my heart or my fate?" (152), "If it's nostalgia, it's nostalgia for a time that didn't exist" (qtd. in Hannaford 36),

> Scraps of identity, a warped & oppressive system that was sidestepped, and I spiralled untangled embracing rushing air & new sensations, fears & opportunities for the rampant imagination. (Doherty, *Books of Albion* 97),

21

"I must record all that excites me & captures my imagination & senses for a second [...] [on] a quest for depth, grace & charm" (19),

> Patting the bedsheet, lightly almost strumming the rhythm on a thigh clad in denim, with a sigh, sad in the diamond mine of the rough soul, dark with glistens of infinite beauty of worth, deep in the imaginary earth (113),

"To distinguish between life and death. But the two are beautiful" (*Albion to Shangri-La* 61), and

> I seem to have spent a lot of my creative time contradicting myself, searching for liberty whilst imprisoning myself. The process of creativity rejuvenates the spirit, it justifies existence; [...] [y]et creativity comes from melancholia [...]. (240)

Whilst these manifestations describe Doherty's perception of his way of living poetry, and this way of living, as it were, can be found to accord with the doctrines of English Romantic poetry[5], he also gives accounts of his understanding of being a poet through music:

> I could live in that song. [...] I understood that, in three minutes you could save the world or find a girl, become anyone, do anything. You could climb mountains or go down sewers. You could drown yourself in your dreams and believe in them. Music made real what I felt deep down in myself without managing to define it, to express it, it was possible. Real. (Doherty qtd. in Black 81)

Doherty depicts here an exaltation of his imagination and his limitless potential in poetic creation which is inarguably reminiscent of the English Romantic doctrines elaborated by Abrams and Bloom. And it seems here that this living creed, this attempt at poetry lived out, not only manifests itself in a Romantic lifestyle Doherty leads, but also in Romantic poetic doctrines that shape the conception of his works. He declares in his diaries that

> it seems to me to be a chase for liberty – reflected in this my reality [...] [.] [P]oetry is divine, the centre & circumference of all estrangement and collect[.] [M]y words are loyal[,] too loyal to my life. They know about the phantoms about me[.] (233)

---

5   see *i. A Definition of English Romantic poetry*

In the words of Yates & Samson, "Pete's obsession with all things romantic and unconventional drove his every move" (39), and Doherty the "pied piper" (280) was inspired to "become the people's poet that the Romantics imagined" (26). Doherty in fact claims a similar inspiration himself in comparing the modern pop-star to the God Pan:

> Pan is a Pixie God... of revelry, music and nature. [...] He's a spiritual survivor from the age before technology. All pop-stars in the modern tradition that capture the imagination of young people especially are Pan-like. [...] Young people still have that complete love for passion and music [...] [, for] their demi-God. The music is like Pan's flute and they go skipping along, chasing the melody into oblivion.
>
> (*Albion to Shangri-La* 248)

In all of Doherty's claims depicted here one can observe a traversing emphasis on the imagination. And it is in this imagination that Hannaford as well as Yates & Samson note Doherty's "quest to discover the meaning of 'Englishness'" (Hannaford 40) and his creation of the "dream of a utopian England" (283) together with his band The Libertines as "champions of the dream; soldiers of the imagination" (283). They acknowledge that this is an imagined England (cf. 93, Yates & Samson 21), which to "a large extent [...] doesn't exist now and didn't exist back then" (Hannaford 40), depicted in "songs that romanticised the environment in which they were living" (60):

> Pete began to adopt an image that conjured up this vision of England, fusing the English gentleman [...] with the crudeness of 1970s punk, the freedom, imagination and disregard for authority of the Romantic poets and occasionally the violence of English soccer hooligans. (43)

This "poetic vision of England" (40) exercised by Doherty is, as Hannaford, Yates & Samson observe, epitomised in his themes of Albion and Arcady. A crucial point to be made here is that all observations and statements taken into account in this sub-chapter are essentially manifestations of Peter Doherty's Romantic public persona. They are claims of a philosophy as well as a living creed, they are expressed not in poems but in claims, yet it is with the themes of Albion and Arcady that Doherty seems to create poetic doctrines strongly in line with those of English Romantic poetry. He offers various accounts and descriptions of these themes in quotes, his overall medial presence and presentation, but he also applies them to his lyrical works. It is the subject of the following sub-chapter to examine Doherty's themes of Albion and Arcady and to place them into literary context so as to follow with the lyric analysis of his songs with regard to all observations made beforehand.

iv. Peter Doherty and his Romantic Poetic Doctrines

(a) Albion

> Albion is the good ship. It's the England we live in. The grey and mundane. The glimpse of the clearing... Arcadia. It's important. It's about melancholy and lust.
>
> (Doherty qtd. in Black 110)

In the statement quoted above, Peter Doherty poignantly outlines his theme of Albion as contemporary England in its function as 'the good ship' on the journey to Arcadia. In fact, his two themes Albion and Arcady appear closely intertwined in their conception, as Albion seemingly acts as the tool with which to achieve the latter goal or destination (cf. Hannaford 43-44). Hannaford notes Albion as the Libertines' "vision of an imaginary England, drawing on the best bits of the past" (43). Placing Doherty's vision of England into cultural and national context, he points to Britain's "crisis of national identity" (40), in which "[p]opular culture has been described as 'the battleground for identity'" (40) (which accords with Morra's observations) and finds that

> [t]o a large extent the England Pete was looking for doesn't exist now and didn't exist back then. His vision of London was opaque, looking at it as he was, through rose-tinted glasses. (40)

"Pete wanted to celebrate England" (92), "ensuring London (and England) [...] would be immortalised in song" (92). Yates & Samson, similarly taking into consideration Doherty's biography as a source for his poetic themes, propose that

> [...] he became obsessed with a handful of key ideas, one of which was a strong concept of Englishness. The rootless youth who wasn't sure where he came from discovered in literature an English ideal that came to replace any precise location. Much of this mythology was borrowed from the Romantic mystic William Blake [...]. In Blake's imagination, the newly industrialised landscape of the late eighteenth century was transformed into a lush, pastoral paradise. [...] Pete took from these

24

ideas, but his Albion ended up radically different from Blake's vision, based mainly in the city rather than the countryside and focusing on its people rather than its landscape […], picking up elements for it in literature, film and television. (20-21)

Suggesting that Doherty's theme of Albion arises from his own rootlessness and thus from the collecting of 'elements' of British literature and culture to assemble a vision of England, Yates & Samson point out here that the focus the Romantic poet placed on England's landscape and countryside finds itself shifted to England's city (specifically London (cf. Hannaford 52)) and its people for Doherty, "forging an idealised inner city as the source of his identity" (Yates & Samson 31).

Doherty employs his theme of Albion not only in philosophy and lifestyle, but also in songs, claiming inter alia: "I have a band (almost) and the spirit of the Albion enthuses it" (*Books of Albion* 8). The Babyshambles album titled "Down in Albion", in which, Hannaford claims, "Pete had laid his soul on tape […] [in] a factual biography of the past year or so" (306), suggests in its title a downward trip into this imaginary England, reminiscent of the metaphorical structure of English Romantic poetry. The song "Albion", released on this album, acts as the lyrical embodiment of Doherty's poetic doctrine of Albion, describing and lionising in detail the imagined England he has in mind – the full examination of which will follow in the lyric analysis.

In his book *Albion: The Origins of the English Imagination*, Peter Ackroyd defines Albion as "not so much a name as the echo of a name" (xix), as in fact an equivalent of "the English imagination [which] takes the form of an endless enchanted circle, or shining ring, moving backwards as well as forwards" (448). Stating that the "English imagination is also syncretic and additive – one episode leading to another episode" (448), Ackroyd delineates a national imagination that is renewed, reformed and reinterpreted endlessly (cf. xix), through which "[d]reams float freely" (51), and which draws both on the past, the present as well as the vision of future – a concept of which Peter Doherty's Albion proves to be a direct example.
So far as concerns English Romantic poetry, Ackroyd propounds that

> [i]n the largest sense romantic literature is the literature of personality, in which the writer imposes upon [a] […] landscape or a […] scene the contours of his or her own preoccupations[.] (437)

This observation is inarguably evocative of the association of Doherty's biography with the development of his poetic doctrine of Albion. Similarly, Ackroyd's account of the English song tradition in earlier centuries carried out by "travelling singers or wandering minstrels" (143) and the therein founded tendency of the "English vision [...] towards the local and the circumstantial" (147) allows to place Doherty's Albion not only within the context of English Romantic poetry as the exultation of the imagination within a visionary national fantasy, but also within that of English imagination and national art itself, especially regarding its syncretic character which fusions various literary and cultural elements into one vision of Albion.

(b) Arcady

> You know – Arcadia? The realm of the infinity? It's a poet's corner. This is the code
> by which we live our lives [...] [,] the pact [...] that turned us all from enemies into
> companions and wayfarers and travellers on the seas of Albion. It's not a cult or a
> religion – it's an awareness of your surroundings; [...] And it's about community and
> pleasure. It came from a whisper through the trees. It came from a crack in the
> pavement. It can also come when you open a bag of crisps, or when you kick a
> football against a goalpost. Even if I was winding you up, it would still be true,
> because Arcadia and the Arcadian Dream is so deep, is so true to our hearts... [...] It
> can be as powerful as your imagination can allow it to be. But, it can also be as dark
> and twisted as your soul... Arcadia encompasses the infinite, and that's why it
> comforts me. (Doherty qtd. in Black 109-110)

Construing here a definition of Arcadia as an interior state of mind characterized as an 'awareness' of the 'infinity' to be found in one's 'surroundings', fuelled, as it were, by the mind's imagination, Doherty in this quote further stresses the contemporary everyday life as a source from which it can arise, or as Hannaford observes:

> For Carl [, Libertines member,] and Pete it didn't have to be in the countryside. Their
> Arcadia could be found in the grimiest parts of the city; they saw beauty in the
> crowded, cold streets of London. But it was still a paradise or utopia, and Pete
> summed it up [...] thus: '*Albion* is our vessel, Arcadia is our destination, and our
> starting point. One needn't have a classical education or a British passport; only an

26

imagination. Let it be what your heart desires, but let not your actions or desires infringe upon the liberty of others.' [...] Arcadia was not in ancient Greece, he insisted, but in the mind, a vision of a better place. (43-44)

Yates & Samson agree that Doherty's theme of Arcadia, though it may be based upon the Greek "rustic paradise" (22), "was a mental state, an attitude to life, rather than a place. Sailing to Arcadia in the *Albion* meant bringing England to the state of liberation he imagined" (22). The state of liberty is here pointed out as a major component of Doherty's Arcadia, "which took the form of a dream world free of rules and restrictions" (22). Within this aspect, Hannaford notes that

> [i]n Pete's Arcadian world, death should not be feared. It is the ultimate freedom – nirvana for a libertine – simply because it is the biggest thing of which 'society' is afraid, because it is the biggest thing it can't control. (319)

Doherty variably refers to either Arcadia or Arcady, and it naturally comes to mind that he in this sense borrows elements from both the Greek pastoral and English poetic connotations (cf. "Arcadia (utopia), "Arcadia"). Hannaford sees in Doherty's and The Libertines' Arcadia an "escapism as their form of protest" (281) against "being constrained by society" (283):

> For The Libertines, their protest was to take their audiences on a journey to Arcadia, their dream of a utopian England found in the back alleys of London, and to find a beauty in its crowded East End markets and in its history. [...] Pete had said back in the very beginning[:] 'We're going to jack it all in and throw ourselves into eternity.' And to join them you only needed an imagination. [...] Carl and Pete were protesting against mediocrity. (283)

Similarly to Doherty's poetic doctrine of Albion, a shift can be observed from the focus on province and nature in the theme of Arcadia in Classical and Renaissance poetry (cf. "Arcadia", "Arcadia (utopia)") to a focus on not only the city and contemporary English culture, but also on the individual mind that is capable, by means of imagination, to reach Doherty's poetic doctrine of Arcadia. In Doherty's own words, he proclaims:

> I do have utopian fantasies, [...] [b]ut they relate more to the imagination and the individual[,] [...] trying to find a way to bridge the gap between that fantasy and

27

reality [...]. (qtd. in Hannaford 33)

Doherty defines the "Arcadian Dream [...] [as] a place in your imagination... a communal imagination" (qtd. in Black 110), declaring that "[f]or three minutes inside a song I can live in Arcadia" (qtd. in 25). It becomes apparent that his Arcadia is much less of an imagined place as it is an achievable state of mind.

John Stevenson suggests in his work that with the emergence of English Romantic poetry

> [...] the pastoral as a convention could no longer exist merely as an artificial exercise but became the source of a new myth from which reality would be perceived – not, as in the past, an appearance of reality. (629)

Stevenson elaborates this 're-settling' of Arcadia in English Romantic poetry by quoting Lynen, who observes that the Romantic movement made it "possible for a poet to write true pastorals within the context of some other mythic rural world" (qtd. in 635) – in Kermode's words: "The object of the pastoral poet's contemplation was no longer merely the happy peasant or shepherd, but the true natural man of the New World" (qtd. in 633). Comparing these Romantic Arcadian doctrines to Doherty's, the resemblance is indisputable, save for the fact that Doherty seemingly 're-settles' Arcadia once more from a rural to an urban mythical world. The 'myth from which reality is perceived', however, can be seen as directly reenacted in Doherty's Arcadia.

Furthermore, as Stevenson evinces that, within English Romantic poetry, the "new myth required not only that the shepherd be in fact a shepherd but that he be a social victim of his world" (635), in other words that the poet "now stands as the type of true innocent; [...] the inspired teacher" (636), in this role nevertheless in "alienation from society" (636), of Doherty it can in comparison on the one hand be said that he shares the doctrine of the poet as 'inspired teacher' of Arcadian visions (where his comparison of the pop-star of today with the God Pan again comes to mind[6]), and that his public persona indeed presents an alienated victim of society (cf. p. 20), yet on the other hand Doherty does not at all stand nor does he claim to stand 'as the type of true innocent' – his Arcadia is no longer focused on pastoral "oneness with nature" (Stevenson 636), but on the utopian state of mind and community summoned by the imagination, by a utopian and idealized dream of Albion.

In conclusion of all that has been observed of Doherty's poetic doctrines of Albion and Arcady, the main attribute that they share with English Romantic poetry as defined in this paper is by all means

6 see p. 23

the exultation of the individual, of the imagination, and their infinite potential. This exultation goes hand in hand with Doherty's cultural and national fantasy, search for infinity and eternity, liberty and stress of the sublimity in the ordinary. Whilst all of these poetic features undoubtedly seem a reenactment of the doctrines of English Romantic poetry, all observations as of yet – those within this paper as well as those made by all considered analysts of Doherty as a Romantic poet – remain based upon claims, statements and propositions which amount to Peter Doherty's Romantic public persona, or in propositions on the literary attributes of his works, yet not based upon literary analyses. Therefore, it is the aim of this paper to now provide within the next chapter a lyric analysis of a selected number of Peter Doherty's lyrics, so as to either found his designation as a Romantic poet upon that analysis – or refute it.

Lyric Analysis[7]

i. Down for the Outing

Peter Doherty's song "Down for the Outing" is a lyric poem in which the lyrical I mourns despair on two levels, in the decline of his individual self as well as of the cultural and national state of Britain, from which he concludes the resolution to exert an outing inside his own mind, promoting this at the end of the poem for all minds of Britain.

To begin with, the title itself suggests an outing to be exerted within the poem that is connected with a downward movement. The reader/hearer is led to expect a pictorial depiction of the announced outing. And the first two of the nine stanzas indeed begin the poem with a very pictorial allegory; the lyrical I, addressing the explicit addressee of these two stanzas (who remains unknown as simply 'you'), gives account of his impression of being deceived by that person as having been sold down a river. Furthermore, he depicts how the addressee suppresses and mocks him by the means of allegorically holding down his timbers in, as it were, the river, and sarcastically interpreting the timbers' drowning and flailing as waving. The abstract concept described by this allegory remains open to interpretation by the reader in its detail (possible interpretations are, for example, the deception by a lover, by a close friend, by a person or even just an entity the lyrical I has trusted, by an institution, etc.), the river quite straightforwardly describes a path the lyrical I has taken and the timbers symbolically denote elements of his character associated with a destroyed ship. The downward movement of the poem as a whole is, in a melancholic and reproachful mood, introduced

7 All lyrics analyzed in this chapter are listed in full in Appendix B.

and stressed here by the repetition of 'down' – as epiphora in lines 1, 3 and 5, as well as immediate repetition at the beginning of line 2. Not only is the lyrical I moving down the flow of the river, the addressee also holds him down as he tries to save himself. Both stanzas are cross rhyming quatrains, likely emphasizing the movement of the river's waves. Doherty's choice of meter is set on iambs, growing from di- (ll. 1-2, 5-6) to trimeter (ll. 3-4, 7-8), yet one stumbles across many alterations, which is naturally due to Doherty's tendency to stress, prolong or omit certain syllables in reciting the lines in song, thereby adhering to the musical beat. This tendency leads to the interpretation that Doherty in this way aims to lay emphasis on the emotion within the poem. The first line, for example, omits the first unstressed syllable, emphasizing the tardiness of the lyrical I's movement down the river. The spondaic substitutions in the third positions of lines 2, 4, 6 and 8 further support the disparity of the timbers' movements among the waves. The enjambments of lines 1-8 are put into contrast to the one-beat pauses Doherty makes at the end of lines 1, 3, 5 and 7, supporting both the flowing movement of the river as well as the lyrical I's timbers' drowning and flailing, driven by the waves.

Then, suddenly, stanza 3 implies a shift of the communicative situation to a dramatic monologue of the lyrical I as he comments on how Britain was somehow saved, yet "raped by all the slaves" (l. 12). Asserting a similarity, the lyrical I now applies the topic of deception, being broken into 'timbers' and suppression to the personified "Britannia" (l. 9), and it is here that Doherty's symbolic conception of England as "the good ship Albion" (qtd. in Hannaford 44) comes to light. The lyrical I, expressing his mourning and despair through, inter alia, onomatopoetic cries of 'Oh' prolonged across 4 beats in lines 9 and 11, gives account of Britain's paradoxical historical situation of having been saved from demise yet at the same time experiencing its downfall in being raped by its slaves. The auxesis of Britain being exploited by means of rape dramatizes the cultural and national decline Britain supposedly undergoes, its 'slaves' here apparently uprising from their own suppression to take revenge. One cannot but interpret the metaphor as a conclusion in the light of historical disappointment to Thomas Arne's "Rule, Britannia", in the sense that 'Britannia' has in fact not become a slave, but is now driven to its demise by the slaves she has subjugated. The otherwise cross rhyming quatrain is expanded by one line in the direct repetition of line 12 in line 13, forming a cinquain and laying further stress upon the lyrical I's mourning of Britain's decline in form of rape. Whilst lines 9 and 11 are sung in free verse, lines 10 and 12, in which the actual account of history takes place, offer metrical structure again in trochaic trimeter, sung in an accelerated rhythm – seemingly underscoring an emotional account, in which a continuously static meter and rhythm cannot be maintained.

Stanzas 4 and 5 return to the personal situation and experience of the lyrical I, who in a reflective mode apologizes to his father in stanza 4 and his mother in stanza 5 for deceiving them, transferring the situation Britain has been depicted in again unto himself. Repeating the meter and rhythm of stanzas 1 and 2, the two quatrains' rhyme scheme is now an inverted Rubaiyat, audibly as well as visually slightly smoothing out the wave movement of stanzas 1 and 2 as well as laying emphasis upon the regret the lyrical I expresses in the apology to his parents. The lyrical I apologizes to the addressed 'Dad' for making the sorrowful situation (simply termed 'it') look even worse by enjoying himself, and in anaphora says 'sorry' to the addressed 'Mum' for giving her hope by doing "good things" (l. 20) in a hopeless situation – all in all apologizing for the inappropriateness of his behaviour. A iambic substitution initiating line 19 inverts the stresses put on the word 'sorry', moving it into particular focus once more. This apology can be interpreted in two ways: as, in fact, the lyrical I's own self-judgment, or as an allegory of Britain's society's inappropriate acting as if there were nothing amiss in its cultural and national state.

The second interpretation as an allegory is accentuated by stanza 6 that follows: the lyrical I here turns to address the educational institutions of England, within another thematic variation accusing them of falsely teaching that 'Britannia' was saved – and in this way reversing his own comment of line 10. The sestett, following the meter and rhythm of stanza 3, brings forth in its latter half the lyrical I's resolution of the outing, the elaboration of which then follows in stanza 7. Uttering again rapidly his emotions, he demands of the British "fool" (l. 24) a sarcastic and imperative "tell me I can live" (l. 25) in iambic trimeter (omitting the first unstressed foot) before expressing in the phrase "ammonia and sieve / my baby's coming with me" (ll. 26-27) his personal resolution of the outing by means of taking drugs, personified as his "baby" and introduced in synecdoche[8]. The ancillary sixth line of this stanza (l. 27), rhyming with none of the lines that precede it, seemingly points out the exodus and retreat the lyrical I exerts from the circumstances that have been depicted in rhyming arrangement.

It is then in stanza 7 that the title of the song is addressed and laid out in further detail. The lyrical I proclaims in dramatic monologue his outing "in the prison of [his] mind" (l. 28) – portraying an inward as well as downward movement from the rejected external world into the realm within his self, within his mind and imagination. The oxymoron of an 'outing' in a 'prison' points metaphorically towards the self's boundaries, its restraint, yet also its protective and zoning character as regards escape from the external world. Arguing that he refuses to conform to social

8   The synecdoche 'ammonia and sieve' describes parts of the process of creating crack cocaine ("TEK").

31

conventions and impositions (depicted in the synecdoche of "three score and ten wreck"[9] (l. 29)), the lyrical I symbolically assesses himself as a lion who will not be blind, nor will he be blindly led by the educational institutions symbolized by the donkey. The extension of the word 'blindly' in its last syllable (implemented in an enjambment of ll. 29 and 30) allows for the rejections of being 'blind' as well as of being 'blindly led' to be taken into account in the lyrical I's declaration. The short tercet consists of a couplet and a final line that constitutes an embracing rhyme with the last line of the preceding stanza 6, thus the poem, having moved away from the cross rhymes of the first stanzas, can be said to establish a parallel relation of content and form, asserting a new rhyme pattern in line with the lyrical I's resolution to go 'down for the outing'. Additionally, spondees dramatically stress the lyrical I's rejective declaration in the beginning of line 29, as well as the accusation of 'schools' as the foolish 'donkey' in spondaic substitution in the fourth position of line 30.

Following this is an empty stanza, in which no words are spoken and the musical instruments play on for the rhythmic equivalent of stanzas 1 and 2 (or 4 and 5). Stanza 8 is a complete repetition of stanza 6, putting again into focus the accusation and resolution asserted by the lyrical I, culminating in the final stanza 9, which provides the conclusion of the poem in a topical variation of stanza 7. A conversion of the lyrical I's resolution into a suggested resolution for the anonymous addressee 'you' can be observed. The monorhyme in the first four lines of the quintet clearly asserts a straightened and smoothened out harmonic mood as opposed to the turbulence at the beginning of the poem, underlining that the solution to the problem has been found – in the "outing in the prison of your mind" (l. 37) now suggested by the lyrical I to be exerted by all minds of Britain. Once more, Doherty applies allegory to delineate the relationship of the individual mind to the external world as well as the process of the 'outing', speaking in line 38 of "pretty ribbons" that cannot bind "a wild beast" – pictorially limning that the free mind of the individual will not allow to be deceived by the enticement of foolish naivety – and in line 39, in parallelism, of "pretty rhythms" that "may ease a troubled mind", promising in the outing through the imagination, which expresses itself in poetry and song, a soothing and consolatory effect. The immediate repetition of "ease a troubled mind" (l. 39) in line 40 and its use in parallelism in line 41 are expressed in trochees, emphasizing the falling, downward movement proposed in the outing. The spondaic substitution in the third position of line 38 seemingly stresses the importance of the 'wild beast' as opposed to the trochaically expressed 'pretty ribbons'. Finally, the lyrical I supports his proposition for the addressee(s) with a comment on the state of contemporary minds in Britain, emphasizing the "many troubled minds round here"

9 'three score and ten' refers to the life span set out in Biblical writings (cf. "The meaning and origin of the expression: Three score and ten").

(l. 41) by means of spondaic substitution for the final syllables.

All in all, it can from this analysis be concluded that Doherty, quite in line with English Romantic poetry, amply uses rhetorical and poetic devices to underline the emotions and content of his song "Down for the Outing". He not only proposes a downward trip into the individual imagination, he also applies his own within the poem in forms of symbolic, allegorical and metaphorical expressions in order to thus portray the decline of Britain's national and cultural state. Besides the main theme of the poem of proclaiming the said outing into the imagination, the theme of disillusionment with historical, cultural and national reality is prominent, as well as Doherty's theme of 'the good ship Albion', here termed 'Britannia'. The internalization of Revolutionary doctrines as exerted by the English Romantic poets can undoubtedly also be brought into connection.

ii. The Ballad of Grimaldi

Peter Doherty's song "The Ballad of Grimaldi" is a narrative ballad which tells the story of the inner conflict of the lyrical I within a love relationship. The title itself rather suggests a story of Joseph Grimaldi, yet the ballad proves to be about the lyrical I, who displays, as it were, a Grimaldian character within the love relationship.

The poem is composed in a mood of argument, within which the lyrical I speaks in personal tones to the explicitly addressed lover. Stanza 1 begins with a request that the lover end the relationship, formulated in a question. The enjambments within the quatrain clash with the pauses Doherty places when singing the lines, undergirding the clash within the depicted relationship in a similar way as the half-rhyme applied in lines 2 and 4. The themes of rejection and fighting establish themselves, underlined also by the applied cross rhyme within the stanza. The trochaic substitution in the fourth position of line 3 sets to music the declared hollowness of the lover's "romance" (l. 3). Furthermore, the spondaic substitutions in the second and third positions of line 4 can be seen to stress the lyrical I's lamenting of the tardiness of the movement depicted in "slowly binding us both" (l. 4). The otherwise prominent trochaic tetrameter (with the exception of iambic pentameter in line 3) and the overall rapid as well as agitated rhythm accessorily underline the lyrical I's upset emotional state.

The same emotional state is observable in stanza 2, where the lyrical I further stresses the futility of their love relationship, using the hyperbole "tell it to the sick and to the damned" (l. 6) to dramatize his position as destroyer of his lover's love and their relationship. The allegory of love crumbling in his hands (cf. l. 8) puts into clear terms what the lyrical I regards as their relationships' hopelessness – his own failure to maintain it. The half-rhyme of lines 6 and 8, the agitated rhythm and the cross rhyme of this quatrain construct the stanza as a logical sequel to the argument begun in stanza 1. Again, spondaic substitutions serve as points of emphasis as well as stresses on the lyrical I's emotional state (cf. the first position in line 5, the final syllables of line 7), and what additionally jumps to attention is a one-beat pause placed in line 7, effecting a suspense as well as tension between the two exclamations it divides, between love and the destruction of it.

Then, the movement and conception of the ballad suddenly changes drastically with stanzas 3 and 4: the rhythm decelerates grandly (which is particularly realized by the musical performance of the song), the rhyme changes from cross rhyme to the actual ballad stanza, and the overall theme changes from fighting argument to recognition of love and hope of reconciliation. Further placed pauses after 'stay' and 'pray' put emphasis on these utterances, giving them temporal room to echo, laying stress upon the hope implied within them. The internal rhymes of the said utterances with line 10's 'say' as well as that of 'pleas' and 'knees' within line 12 echo the lyrical I's desire for harmony and connection to the addressed lover. In connection to the act of praying, the biblical reference 'St. Jude' is introduced as symbol for the lyrical I's hope in light of hopelessness[10]. Stanza 4 concomitantly provides a clear syntactical parallelism of lines 13 and 15 as well as 14 and 16, further stressing the longing for harmony. Supportingly, the final word 'adore' in lines 13 and 15 is each time prolonged across 2 beats.

Stanza 5 returns to the agitated rhythm, meter and rhyme of the first two stanzas, and the lyrical I returns to depicting his and his lover's argument. He here employs the simile of Grimaldi[11] to describe his two-sided and paradoxical behaviour in the love relationship, both laughing and falling. His lover is attributed the simile of Baby Jane[12], thereby characterizing her role in the love relationship as a disappointed, unsuccessful, openly violent and reality-denying partner. In light of their futility, the lyrical concludes stanza 5 with the use of irony, encouraging his lover to tell him again the "promising lies" (l. 19). An assonance observable for 'fall' (l. 17) and 'promising' (l. 19) inwardly links the said promise to the downfall of their relationship.

---

10 cf. "Who is St. Jude?".
11 Joseph Grimaldi was a pantomime clown who spearheaded the notion of the pantomime clown as a combination of "rogue and simpleton criminal and innocent dupe in one character [...] [, along with] impudent thievery" ("Joseph Grimaldi").
12 cf. "What Ever Happened To Baby Jane?".

In stanza 6, the lyrical I changes the communicative situation from argumentative dialogue with the addressed lover to a dramatic monologue, giving account of his experience with fear and hope by means of the allegory of having "walked these streets all of [his] life" (l. 21). Following this, the lyrical I moves from appearing explicitly to becoming implicit within the poem, from line 23 onwards telling the story of two lovers in 3rd person narrative. The paradox that the depicted 'she' "took him to Stepney and made him a wife" (l. 23) points out that the woman is in fact the ruling force within the love relationship. The lyrical I's distancing from the whole story, though, leaves open to interpretation whether the love relationship depicted in this stanza is the same as that depicted in the stanzas before. The negatively connoted 'Stepney' as degenerated[13] acts as an allegory to go hand in hand with the character of the love relationship. The further allegory of crashing and burning in line 24 pictorially describes the lovers' predicted demise, whereupon stanza 7 syntactically repeats stanza 2, maintaining the shift of perspective and narrative from 'I' and 'you' to 'he' and 'she'. In the end, it can be observed that the lyrical I offers no conclusion or solution to his inner conflict within his love relationship, but instead withdraws from its account as agent, choosing to become narrator of a story distanced from his self.

Bearing in mind all that has been observed, "The Ballad of Grimaldi" further shows Doherty's emphasis on poetic openness to emotion, relating form to content, as well as his inclination to reference in rhetorical form elements of British as well as international cultural history, of the Bible and of contemporary London, which makes this poem inter alia an execution of his fusing of elements of British culture and literature into his own poetic doctrine of national celebration.

iii. Albion

The Babyshambles' song "Albion" is inarguably Peter Doherty's embodiment of his poetic doctrine of Albion in poetry and song. It is the explicit implementation of his cultural nationalism and celebration of a visionary, imaginary England in manifold pictorial allegories and symbols. Drawing on very concrete images found in contemporary England as well as listing English toponyms, Doherty composes an ode to his vision of Albion very much in the line of the Pindaric character of richness in metaphor and "intensely emotive language" ("Pindaric ode").

The lyrical I begins in stanza 1 with the phrase "Down in Albion" (l. 1), suggesting a downward

13 cf. "Stepney".

movement when going there. He addresses the explicit yet anonymous addressee 'you', in a directly communal manner also as 'we' – therein including himself. The metaphorical "black and blue" (l. 2), violent and rogue character of Albion's inhabitants is acknowledged, but immediately set aside by the lyrical I, who then preaches that he'd rather like to talk about English origin and personal feelings, expressing this in questions (cf. ll. 4-5). The direct repetition in epiphora of 'talk about that' in lines 3 and 6 lays emphasis upon the distinction and preference of subject when talking of Albion that the lyrical I here evinces, and in the same manner so does the repetitive rhyme scheme 'abc abc' within the sestet.

In stanza 2, the lyrical then begins to extensively elaborate on what he wants to talk about, applying various allegories and symbols that constitute Doherty's myth of Albion, elevating rather simple, crude and lower-class elements the likes of "gin in teacups" (l. 8) and "violence in bus stops" (l. 10) to connotations of beauty and sources of sublime national fantasy, which is accentuated by the cross rhyming quatrain these allegories are constructed in, implying a harmonious correlation very much like the hymn. Stanza 3 provides direct repetitions of the 2nd stanza's lines 8 and 9 in its own lines 12 and 13, as well as parallelism of lines 10 and 11 in lines 14 and 15, further emphasizing the grand design of all of the depicted elements as a whole myth of Albion. In both stanzas, the spondaic substitution in the final positions of lines 10 and 14 lay stress upon the words 'bus stops' and 'dole queues' and thus upon the beauty to be seen in elements of simple, contemporary everyday life in Britain. The final spondee in line 15, resulting in a prolonged 'checkout' across 3 beats, inter alia emphasizes the passion the lyrical I sees in these phrases.

Stanza 4, rhyming in ballad form, contains the lyrical I's explicit readdressing of the addressee in offering to meet him/her if he/she is searching for what the lyrical I goes on to depict as the "cheap sort set in false anticipation" (ll. 16-17), the common, sinful and rogue inhabitant of Britain that he is. In stanza 5, he then concludes in inviting the addressee to "come away" (l. 20) with him, the repetition of which within the same line suggests an importance in having to 'come away' instead of already being in Albion as an inhabitant of Britain – it is the trip via the imagination that the lyrical I is here inviting the addressee to embark on. Doherty freely makes use of meter and line length throughout this poem, which is especially manifested in the trochaic, line-prolonging listing of English toponyms beginning in line 22. Following the listing, the stanza's final phrase "Anywhere in Albion" (l. 23) introduces a lyric pause of 16 beats, presumably pointing towards the list as being endless, or even Albion as being an endless, infinite realm – the listener of the song is invited to let the said phrase ring in his mind for the whole 16 beats that follow (which is furthermore stressed in

36

other band members' repeating of the phrase).

Stanzas 6 and 7 continue the poem with further symbolical depictions in impure quintets with embracing rhymes applied in lines 25 and 28 as well as in lines 30 and 33, again stressing correlation. A striking feature in these stanzas is the amalgamation of contemporary and historical cultural as well as national elements of Britain, performed in the parallelism of 'Yellowing classics' in line 24 and 'Reebok classics' in line 29. Further repetitions of lines 25 in 30 and 28 in 33 lay further emphasis upon a nostalgic national celebration in 'cannons at dawn' and 'an English song'. In fact, the stanzas 8-9 and 10-11 that follow each prove to be, paired as such, parallel repetitions of stanzas 4-5. Once more, metrical substitution is used to stress the passion within a word or phrase, most significantly shown in the final foot of line 40, 'Newcastle', where all three syllables are stressed by means of a spondaic substitution within the dactyl. To close the poem, stanza 12 consists of the immediately repetitive monorhyming quatrain, simply repeating 'Anywhere in Albion'.

All in all, it can be concluded that "Albion" proves to be a direct exertion of Doherty's poetic doctrine of Albion in content as well as form, the latter repeatedly emphasizing the elevation of the symbolic and allegorical cultural national elements within the poem. The passion related by the lyrical I to these elements is stressed in repetition and use of parallelism, the same is in this way done regarding the invitation to embark on the imaginary trip down in Albion. And furthermore, "Albion" also proves to be Yates & Samson's observation of Doherty's focus on England's people within his theme of Albion (cf. 21) manifested in poetry.

iv. The Good Old Days

The Libertines' song "The Good Old Days" is a 5-stanza lyric poem in which the lyrical I explains that the 'good old days' of English culture are in fact not in the past, but in the present, appealing to the imagination to set sail on the ship Albion.
The first stanza, composed in ballad form, introduces the contemporary English people's spiritual heritage from "Queen Boadicea" (l. 1), referencing in allegory a spirit of nationalism (cf. "Boudicca"). The trochaic substitution as well as threefold immediate repetition of 'children' in line 3 lays emphasis upon a relative proximity within the said heritage as well as upon the English people as Boadicea's children.

In the following second stanza, the lyrical I goes on to proclaim that the explicitly addressed addressee (an anonymous 'you') should not lose his/her "faith in love and music" (l. 5), as this would result in the lyrical I's own loss of faith (cf. l. 7). The cross rhyming quatrain stresses the correlation of lyrical I and you, supported by an unchanging trochaic pentameter in lines 5 and 7 as well as a constant trimeter of one anapest embraced by two single stresses.

Stanza 3 provides the lyrical I's account of how he wants to avoid repeating the past by metaphorical means of "falling back into [his] bad old ways" (l. 10), complaining that it allegorically "chars" (l. 11) his heart when the addressee calls for 'the good old days', and this charring is further put into focus by means of internal rhyme. The lyrical I argues in the parallelisms of lines 13 and 14 that the said 'good old days' in the past do not exist, insisting upon creating new ones today.

This personal account is by means of variation converted into a cultural and national topic in stanzas 4-5. In further allegories, the lyrical I proclaims that the negatively connoted state of British society is not what can be considered 'the good old days' (cf. ll. 15-17). Instead, the lyrical I recalls symbols such as "daisy chains and schoolyard games" (l. 18) and "a list of things we said we'd do tomorrow" (l. 19) as the contributors to the said 'good old days', the immediate repetition of the latter stressing its importance further. In addition, whilst stanza 4 is initially played in a slow rhythm and contains caesura in lines 15 and 18, the said repetition in line 20 rhythmically leads back on to the meter and rhythm of stanza 2, now constructing the final fifth stanza, in which the lyrical I now fully turns the theme of nostalgia for the past refocused unto today into his conclusion of cultural and national exultation of Britain by means of the imagination. While the "Arcadian Dream has all fallen through" (l. 21), allegorically denoting that utopia cannot be found in the deceptive degenerative contemporary state of British society, the lyrical I states that consolation lies within the imagination's power to envision this utopia within contemporary Britain, and this is underlined by the strongly symbolic poetic language used within the stanza, describing the imaginative journey by means of maritime terms, referencing the contemporary cultural diversity within Britain by means of the metaphor "twelve rude boys on the oars" (l. 25)[14]. Finally, the additional repetitive line "In the good old days" (l. 26) lays further stress upon the poem's conclusion that 'the good old days' can be found in a nostalgic view of today.

---

14 cf. "Rude boy".

Conclusion

This bachelor paper has examined Peter Doherty's public persona, his poetic doctrines and a selected number of his song lyrics in order to answer the question whether he can or cannot be termed a Romantic poet.

The definition of English Romantic poetry has provided the basis for the examination by asserting it as an ongoing literary and artistic development that nevertheless bears concrete definitions in set poetic doctrines. The propositions considered in the adjacent sub-chapter have brought into connection English Romantic poetry and contemporary popular rock music regarding their shared roles in different points of history as signifiers and expressions "of contemporary national identity" (Morra 10) as well as regarding the heritage of English Romantic poetry in rock music in the form of "vulgar Romantic pantheism" (Pattison 29) and its reinterpretation as a "living creed" (38), thus justifying the examination and analysis of a contemporary rock star for elements of English Romantic poetry.

The examination of Peter Doherty's public persona has shown that Doherty in fact proclaims this Romantic living creed, attempting to "live out the poetry" (*Move* qtd. in *Books of Albion* 132) that he writes. In retrospect, it might formally have been more helpful to combine the definition of Romantic poetic doctrines and Doherty's in one chapter so as to view the direct comparison at hand, though the argumentative structure of this paper nevertheless logically leads on each chapter by establishing the preceding ones as bases for the further examination.

The outlining of Peter Doherty's Romantic poetic doctrines of Albion and Arcady has brought forth that they indeed resemble English Romantic poetic doctrines, especially with regard to the exaltation of the imagination, of the individual, of limitlessness in potential, and of the visionary character the poet assumes, alongside the quest for infinity and eternity, the stress on sublimity in the ordinary, the nostalgia in a passionate, symbol-laden imaginative world drawing on history as well as contemporary life, the internalization of Revolutionary doctrines and the use of metaphorical structures aimed downward and inward. But it has also brought forth the observation that Doherty's Romantic doctrines are implied in a living creed and not in his lyric works, which gave way to the following lyric analysis.

And finally, that lyric analysis has shown that Peter Doherty indeed applies Romantic poetic doctrines, attributes and literary features in his lyrics. His main focus is on the imagination as a means to escape reality, as a means to establish a visionary Romantic poetic world by "cellotaping together loads of dilettantes fantasies" (Doherty, *Books of Albion* 132).

39

Bearing all of these findings in mind, it can be concluded that it appears coherent and logical to term Peter Doherty an English Romantic poet on account of the fact that he shares their poetic doctrines in living creed as well as lyrical works. Supporting this aspect is Chandler & McLane's observation that

> [...] Romantic poetry, however deeply rooted in its historical and cultural moment, also remains 'ever more about to be,' in Wordsworth's phrase – ever ready to be reactivated and reimagined by the latest reader. (8)

Yet it is here that one must also take into account another observation by the same authors:

> [...] the adjective 'Romantic' denotes not just a period, but a style, a movement, a way of thinking (an 'ideology', some have said), even a way of being in the world. [...] Poets writing long after the Battle of Waterloo might well think of themselves as 'in the Romantic line.' (3)

Peter Doherty shares his poetic doctrines with English Romantic poetry – but not entirely. He modifies them to creative his own poetic doctrines 'in the Romantic line', turning towards the people and the city of London instead of the British nature and landscape to form his themes of Albion and Arcady. Ultimately he proves to offer in his works more than a Romantic public persona and more than the heritage of vulgar pantheism and cultural nationalism delineated by Pattison and Morra. Doherty has created poetic doctrines of sublimity in contemporary England, of a "communal imagination" (Doherty qtd. in Black 110). Yates & Samson see him as "the people's poet that the Romantics imagined" (26). The answer to the question whether Peter Doherty can be termed a Romantic poet therefore depends on how one defines English Romantic poetry. If one defines it as an infinitely ongoing movement, Peter Doherty can undoubtedly be termed one of its main lyrical bearers. If one defines it as a literary period that leaves its marks up until today, Peter Doherty can be termed as a musical poet strongly 'in the Romantic line'. The definition of English Romantic poetry as well as the further observations within this bachelor paper indeed allow the former.

Figure 1. Cover image of Babyshambles' "Shotter's Nation".

Appendix B – Lyrics

Note: The lyrics listed in this appendix are presented according to their original presentation where available, the sources of which are noted at the foot of each lyric. Where an original written source from Doherty or his bands is not available, the presentation here follows the examples of UptheAlbion.com, the fan-based Libertines and Babyshambles online encyclopedia, or other similar sources. Alterations to sources are made at the author's own discretion when seen to be more according to the poetical structure.

For the sake of structural overview and unity, the lyrics are laid out individually per page.

i. Down for the Outing

Slowly down
down the river
the one you sold me down
where all my timbers shiver

You hold them down
and as they're flailing
yes as they drown
you say, "Oh look, they're waving"

Oh, Britannia
somehow she was saved
Oh, Britannia
raped by all the slaves
raped by all the slaves and

Sorry Dad
for every single
good time that I had
They made it look so bad

Sorry Mum
sorry for all the
good things that I've done
gave you hope when there was none

Schools how can you
say that we were saved
Fool, oh Britannia
tell me I can live
ammonia and sieve
my baby's coming with me

for the outing in the prison of my mind
I'm no 3 score and 10 wreck I won't be blind
-ly led, this lion by a donkey

Schools how can you
say that we were saved
Fool, oh Britannia
tell me I can live
ammonia and sieve
my baby's coming with me

Down for the outing in the prison of your mind
where pretty ribbons a wild beast cannot bind
and pretty rhythms may ease a troubled mind
ease a troubled mind
many troubled minds round here[1]

---

1   An as of yet unreleased song, the lyrics of "Down for the Outing" are based on their presentation in the Youtube
    video "Peter Doherty – Down For The Outing (Lyrics Video)" uploaded by Enes Dolovac as well as their
    presentation on UptheAlbion.com.

ii. The Ballad of Grimaldi

While there's still a fighting chance
Can't you just get up and go
And get away from this hollow romance
It's slowly binding us both

Because you'll tell me what you want and I'll avoid it
Tell it to the sick and to the damned
Show me what you love, watch me destroy it
For love just crumbles in my hands

But if you stay for a while
I'll try to think of something kind to say
Maybe if we pray for a while
St Jude might hear my pleas and see me on my knees

Because she knows I adore you
We won't be fighting again tonight
Not if she knows I adore you
There won't be fighting in the streets

I laugh and fall just like Grimaldi
You wear make-up like Baby Jane
All of those promising lies that you told me
Come on and tell me them again

Oh well, I walked these streets all of my life
The fear and hope at every turn
She took him to Stepney and made him a wife
Oh yeah you know they'll crash and burn

Because she tells him what she wants and he avoids it
Tell it to the sick and to the damned
Show him what you love, watch him destroy it
For love seems to crumble in his hands[2]

---

2 "The Ballad of Grimaldi" is released on Peter Doherty's single "Broken Love Song" (2009). The presentation of its lyrics here are based upon that on UptheAlbion.com.

iii. Albion

Down in Albion
They're black and blue
But we don't talk about that
Are you from 'round here?
How do you do?
I'd like to talk about that

Talk over
Gin in teacups
And leaves on the lawn
Violence in bus stops
And a pale thin girl with eyes forlorn

Gin in teacups
And leaves on the lawn
Violence in dole queues
And a pale thin girl behind the checkout

But if you're looking for a cheap sort
Set in false anticipation
I'll be waiting in the photo booth
Of the underground station

So come away, won't you come away
We could go to
Deptford, Catford, Watford, Digberth, Mansfield
Anywhere in Albion

Yellowing classics
And cannons at dawn
Coffee wallahs
Pith helmets
And an English song

Reebok classics
And cannons at dawn
Terrible warlords
Good warlords
And an English song

But if you're looking for a cheap tart
All glint with perspiration
There's a four mile queue
Outside the disused power station

Now come away, won't you come away
We'll go to
Satsworth, Senford, Weovil, Woomoyle, Newcastle
Oh anywhere

If you are looking for a cheap tart
All glint with perspiration
There's a five mile queue
Outside the disused power station

Now come away, won't you come away
We'll go to
Bedtown, Oldham, Nunthorpe, Rowlam, Bristol
Anywhere in Albion

Anywhere in Albion
Anywhere in Albion
Anywhere in Albion
Anywhere in Albion[3]

---

3   "Albion" is released on the Babyshambles album "Down in Albion" (2005). The presentation of its lyrics here are based upon that in Doherty's *Books of Albion* (207-208) as well as that on UptheAlbion.com.

iv. The Good Old Days

If Queen Boadicea
Is long dead and gone
Still then the spirit in her children's children's children
It lives on

If you've lost your faith in love and music
The end won't be long
Because if it's gone for you I too may lose it
And that would be wrong

I try so hard to keep myself from falling
B into my bad old ways
And it chars my heart to always hear you calling
Calling for the good old days
Because there were no good old days
These are the good old days

It's not about tenements and needles
And all the evils in their eyes
And the backs of their minds
Daisy chains and schoolyard games
And a list of things we said we'd do tomorrow
List of things we said we'd do tomorrow

The Arcadian Dream has all fallen through
But the Albion sails on course
So let's man the decks and hoist the rigging
Because the pig man's found the source
And there's twelve rude boys on the oars

In the good old days[4]

---

4   "The Good Old Days" is released on The Libertines' album "Up The Bracket" (2002). The presentation of its lyrics here are based upon that in Doherty's *Books of Albion* (9) as well as that on UptheAlbion.com.

Appendix C – Doherty Discography

Note: This discography excludes the exclusively live releases "Oh What A Lovely Tour – Babyshambles Live" and "Live at Nancy – Spotify Exclusive" in order to avoid repeatedly listing songs already completely listed in other releases.

Albums

The Libertines – Up The Bracket (2002)
1. Vertigo
2. Death on the Stairs
3. Horrorshow
4. Time For Heroes
5. Boys in the Band
6. Radio America
7. Up the Bracket
8. Tell the King
9. The Boy Looked At Johnny
10. Begging
11. The Good Old Days
12. I Get Along

The Libertines – The Libertines (2004)
1. Can't Stand Me Now
2. Last Post on the Bugle
3. Don't Be Shy
4. The Man Who Would Be King
5. Music When the Lights Go Out
6. Narcissist
7. The Ha Ha Wall
8. Arbeit Macht Frei
9. Campaign of Hate
10. What Katie Did
11. Tomblands
12. The Saga
13. Road to Ruin
14. What Became of the Likely Lads
15. France

Babyshambles – Down in Albion (2005)
1. La Belle et la Bête
2. Fuck Forever
3. A'rebours
4. The 32nd of December
5. Pipedown
6. Sticks and Stones
7. Killamangiro
8. 8 Dead Boys
9. In Love with a Feeling
10. Pentonville
11. What Katy Did Next
12. Albion
13. Back from the Dead
14. Loyalty Song
15. Up The Morning
16. Merry Go Round

Other

The Libertines – What a Waster (2002)
1. What a Waster
2. I Get Along
3. Mayday

The Libertines – Up the Bracket (2002)
1. Up the Bracket
2. The Delaney
3. Plan A

The Libertines – Time For Heroes (2003)
1. Time For Heroes
2. General Smuts – Demo Version
3. Bangkok – Demo Version

The Libertines – Don't Look Back Into The Sun (2003)
1. Don't Look Back Into the Sun
2. Death on the Stairs
3. Tell The King – Original Demo Version

The Libertines – Can't Stand Me Now (2004)
1. Can't Stand Me Now
2. Cyclops
3. Dilly Boys

The Libertines – Can't Stand Me Now (2004)
1. Can't Stand Me Now
2. Never Never

The Libertines – What Became of the Likely Lads (2004)
1. What Became of the Likely Lads
2. Skag and Bone Man – Live Version
3. Time For Heroes – Live Version

The Libertines – What Became of the Likely Lads (2004)
1. What Became of the Likely Lads
2. The Delaney – Live Version

Babyshambles – Killamangiro (2004)
1. Killamangiro
2. The Man Who Came To Stay

Babyshambles – Black Boy Lane (2005)
1. Black Boy Lane

Babyshambles – Shotter's Nation (2007)
1. Carry On Up The Morning
2. Delivery
3. You Talk
4. Unbilotitled
5. Side of the Road
6. Crumb Begging Baghead
7. Unstookie Titled
8. French Dog Blus
9. There She Goes
10. Baddie's Boogie
11. Deft Left Hand
12. Lost Art of Murder

The Libertines – Time For Heroes – The Best of The Libertines (2007)
1. Up the Bracket
2. Time For Heroes
3. Mayday
4. Don't Look Back Into The Sun
5. Tell The King
6. What Katy Did
7. Can't Stand Me Now
8. What a Waster
9. The Delaney
10. Boys in the Band
11. Death on the Stairs
12. I Get Along
13. What Became of the Likely Lads

Peter Doherty – Grace/Wastelands (2009)
1. Arcady
2. Last of the English Roses
3. 1939 Returning
4. A Little Death Around the Eyes
5. Salome
6. I Am The Rain
7. Sweet By And By
8. Palace of Bone
9. Sheepskin Tearaway
10. Broken Love Song
11. New Love Grows on Trees
12. Lady Don't Fall Backwards

Babyshambles – F**k Forever (2005)
1. F**k Forever
2. East of Eden
3. Babyshambles

Babyshambles – F**k Forever (2005)
1. F**k Forever
2. Monkey Casino

Babyshambles – F**k Forever (Clean Version) (2005)
1. F**k Forever – Clean Edit

Babyshambles – Albion (2005)
1. Albion – Single Version
2. Clementine
3. Why Did You Break My Heart / Piracy

Babyshambles – Albion (2005)
1. Albion – Single Version
2. Do You Know Me

Babyshambles – The Blinding EP (2006)
1. The Blinding
2. Love You But You're Green
3. I Wish
4. Beg, Steal or Borrow
5. Sedative

Babyshambles – Delivery (2007)
1. Delivery
2. Stone Me
3. I Wish – Mik's Vocal Version
Note: 2 other releases of "Delivery" are excluded here as they contain but further versions of the song "Delivery"

Babyshambles – You Talk (2007)
1. You Talk
2. Revelations
3. UnBiloTitled – Acoustic Version
4. Carry On Up The Morning – Acoustic Version
Note: 9 other releases of "You Talk" are excluded here as they contain but further versions of the song "You Talk"

Peter Doherty – Last of the English Roses (2009)
1. Last of the English Roses
2. Through The Looking Glass
3. Don't Look Back

Babyshambles – Sequel to the Prequel (2013)
1. Fireman
2. Nothing Comes to Nothing
3. New Pair
4. Farmer's Daughter
5. Fall from Grace
6. Maybelline
7. Sequel to the Prequel
8. Dr. No
9. Penguins
10. Picture Me in a Hospital
11. Seven Shades
12. Minefield
13. Cuckoo
14. Stranger In My Own Skin
15. The Very Last Boy Alive
16. After Hours

Peter Doherty – Broken Love Song (2009)
1. Broken Love Song
2. The Ballad of Grimaldi

Babyshambles – Nothing Comes to Nothing (2013)
1. Nothing Comes to Nothing
2. Picture Me in a Hospital – Demo

Babyshambles – Fall From Grace (2013)
1. Fall From Grace
2. Bundles

Peter Doherty – Flags of the Old Regime (2015)
1. Flags of the Old Regime
2. Dust on the Road

Bibliography

Primary sources

Babyshambles. *Down in Albion*. Rough Trade, 2005. CD.

---. "Albion". *Down in Albion*.

Battersby, Matilda. "Pete Doherty: I was a bit unhinged". *The Independent*. The Independent, 17 Feb. 2012. Web. 8 Apr. 2015.

Black, Dave. *Pete Doherty "Talking": Pete Doherty In His Own Words*. London: Omnibus Press, 2006. Print.

B Libertines. "Arena – Peter Doherty (full documentary)". Online video clip. *Youtube*. Youtube, 18 Dec. 2013. Web. 11 Jan. 2015.

Doherty, Peter. *From Albion to Shangri-La: Journals 2008-2013*. Ed. Nina Antonia. London: Thin Man Press, 2014. Print.

---. *The Books of Albion*. London: Orion, 2009. Print.

Enes Dolovac. "Peter Doherty – Down For The Outing (Lyrics Video)". Online video clip. *Youtube*. Youtube, 12 July 2012. Web. 8 Apr. 2015.

"Pete Doherty Live Acoustic Show (First Set): Brixton Jamm presents...". *Jamm*. N.p., n.d. Web. 17 Feb. 2015.

Peter Doherty. "The Ballad of Grimaldi". *Broken Love Song*. Parlophone, 2009. 7" Vinyl, Digital Download.

The Libertines. "The Good Old Days". *Up The Bracket*. Rough Trade, 2002. CD.

UptheAlbion.com. N.p., 2015. Web. 11 Apr. 2015.

Secondary sources

Ackroyd, Peter. *Albion: The Origins of the English Imagination*. London: Chatto & Windus, 2002. Print.

"Arcadia". *A Dictionary of Literary Terms and Literary Theory*. 5th ed. 2013. Print.

"Arcadia (utopia)". *Wikipedia*. Wikipedia, n.d. Web. 13 Apr. 2015.

Bloom, Harold, ed. *English Romantic Poetry*. Broomall, PA: Chelsea House Publishers, 2004. Print.

---. Introduction. By Bloom. Bloom 1-23.

"Boudicca". *Encyclopedia Britannica Online*. N.d. Web. 14 Apr. 2015.

Chandler, James, and Maureen N. McLane, eds. *The Cambridge Companion to British Romantic Poetry*. Cambridge: Cambridge University Press, 2008. Print.

---. Introduction. By Chandler and McLane. Chandler and McLane 1-9.

"Charles Baudelaire". *Encyclopedia Britannica Online*. N.d. Web. 8 Apr. 2015.

Day, Adrian. *Romanticism*. London: Routledge, 1996. Print.

Goodman, Kevis. "Romantic poetry and the science of nostalgia." Chandler and McLane 195-216.

Hannaford, Alex. *Pete Doherty: Last of the Rock Romantics*. London: Ebury Press, 2007. Print.

"Joseph Grimaldi". *Encyclopedia Britannica Online*. N.d. Web. 14 Apr. 2015.

Meyer, Michael. *English and American Literatures*. Tübingen and Basel: A. Francke Verlag, 2008. Print.

Morra, Irene. *Britishness, popular music, and national identity: the making of modern Britain*. New York: Routledge, 2014. Print.

O'Flinn, Paul. *How to Study Romantic Poetry*. 2nd ed. Basingstoke: Palgrave, 2001. Print.

Pattison, Robert. *The Triumph of Vulgarity: Rock Music in the Mirror of Romanticism*. New York: Oxford University Press, 1987. Print.

"Pindaric ode". *Encyclopedia Britannica Online*. N.d. Web. 14 Apr. 2015.

"Romantic and Postromantic Poetics." *The New Princeton Encyclopedia of Poetry and Poetics*. 3rd ed. 1993. Print.

"Romanticism." *Encyclopedia Britannica Online*. N.d. Web. 20 Jan. 2015.

"Romanticism." *Merriam-Webster's Collegiate Dictionary*. 11th ed. 2003. *Merriam-Webster Online*. N.d. Web. 25 Jan. 2015.

"Romantik, das Romantische." *Historisches Wörterbuch der Philosophie.* 1992. Print.

"Rude boy". *Wikipedia.* Wikipedia, n.d. Web. 14 Apr. 2015

"Stepney". *Wikipedia.* Wikipedia, n.d. Web. 14 Apr. 2015.

Stevenson, John. "Arcadia Re-Settled: Pastoral Poetry and Romantic Theory". *Studies in English Literature, 1500-1900.* Vol. 7, No. 4, Nineteenth Century. pp. 629-638. Autumn: Rice University, 1967. Print.

Stewart, Susan. "Romantic meter and form." Chandler and McLane 53-75.

"TEK – questions about some details in creating base with ammonia". *Drugs-Forum.* SIN Foundation, 2002-2003. Web. 14 Apr. 2015.

"Thomas Arne". *Encyclopedia Britannica Online.* N.d. Web. 14 Apr. 2015.

"The meaning and origin of the expression: Three score and ten". *The Phrase Finder.* Gary Martin, 1990-2015. Web. 14 Apr. 2015.

Wainwright, Jeffrey. *Poetry: The Basics.* London and New York: Routledge, 2004. Print.

"What Ever Happened To Baby Jane?". *Encyclopedia Britannica Online.* N.d. Web. 14 Apr. 2015.

"Who is St. Jude?". *The National Shrine of Saint Jude.* The Claretians, 2015. Web. 14 Apr. 2015.

Wordsworth, Jonathan and Jessica Wordsworth, eds. *The New Penguin Book of Romantic Poetry.* London: Penguin Books, 2001. Print.

---. Introduction: The Romantic Period. By Wordsworth and Wordsworth. Wordsworth and Wordsworth xxvii-xlviii.

---. Preface. By Wordsworth and Wordsworth. Wordsworth and Wordsworth xxiii-xxvi.

Wu, Duncan, ed. *Romanticism: an anthology.* 3rd ed. Walden: Blackwell Publishing, 2006. Print.

---. Introduction. By Wu. Wu xxix-xlii.

Yates, Nathan, and Pete Samson. *Pete Doherty: on the edge, the true story of a troubled genius.* London: John Blake, 2005. Print.

Ingram Content Group UK Ltd.
Milton Keynes UK
UKHW040640230523
422205UK00004B/174

9 783656 966876